Dedication

To my beautiful wife Thèrése
And daughters, Hannah, Bridgette, Jamie

Without your support I would never been able to
complete it.

Thank You

Table of Contents

Table of Contents

Preface

I started writing this book as a way to keep what was left of my sanity. Watching over and over as people go to the poles, vote then complain about the politician they elected not doing what they said they would. That is the definition of insanity, doing the same thing over and over, yet expecting a different result. That doesn't work, yet every election cycle, whether it is local, State or Federal, the same thing happens over and over again. I get it people get comfortable with one political party; they listen to their, priest's ministers, rabbis, mullahs and so on. We listen to family, take on a tradition of voting one way or another, we join a union, public or private and they voice support and spend dues to push for a specific candidate. Corporations create Political Action Committees or PACs and ask workers to contribute and on and on it goes...

Were becoming part of a heard, that mentality that will cost you your freedoms at some point. People have gone from thinking for themselves to group think, a hive mentality that were all the same, we all work the same we all are the same and that is a lie. Were not the same, each person is unique, from their DNA to their fingerprints. We each react differently under the same stimuli and yet, group think or in the case of voting, you can call it traditionalism, which is a form of group think. My Great grandfather always voted for this political party, so did my grandfather and my father so I must continue the tradition. It's a form of group think; it's also a form of insanity. Doing the same thing over and over, expecting different results.

Preface

Voting for the same party over and over no matter what, is not doing yourself or your country a service. It's looking out for the political party's interest plain and simple. You're playing right into their hands no matter which party it is. They both promise you the world, tell you what you want to here and you continue to vote for them perpetuating the problems they fail to solve over and over. It may not be you're guy, he may be great, maybe he can walk on water, but until all the politicians get the message that they're replaceable, that they do our work, not the work of special interests, Unions, Corporations, Billionaires, Millionaires, nor the very parties they belong to, until they get the message they report to all of us, they have to be replaced. Ask yourself, when did politics become a full time job? When we stopped paying attention and voting them out, we allowed politicians to change a call to service to a job and a life time income.

I try my hardest; I look at the politician, check the voting records, look at what they offer then and only then vote. Have I been disappointed, let's just say the last president has been a huge disappointment for me. Did I vote for him, yes in 2007, did I do it again in 2011 no and give the chance to go back and change my first vote I would. There are many reasons why, same with other political candidates. None of them not one that I know of thinks outside the government box, they get elected and it seems any good idea is thrown out and only more money can solve the problem.

Preface

Here's something only a politician could believe "Government can solve all our problems if it taxes enough". They could collect ever dollar an American makes, redistribute it so we all make the same amount of money and guess what, they'd exclude themselves from paying in not from collecting.

We've allowed them to become a fifth estate. They rule, expand government, tax and spend like a sailor on shore leave for the first time in years and leave us with the mess. Trying doing that with your credit cards, ask the bank to up the available credit every time you get close to the limit, you'll pay it back, you're good for the money.. In government, they do exactly that, vote to raise the debt ceiling and who gets to pay for it? Not them, not us, but generations from now someone will.

The main problem here is that more government has never solved any problem. It's caused problems. When government gets involved cost rise three to five times more than they should.   It adds time to fixing any problem you have. At any level of government the time it takes from the submission of a request to the end takes entirely too long, they'll say its due diligence. No its breaks and work load reduction, regulations and any number of other things they can do to slow process. See slowing the process allows them to say they're underfunded, under staffed so they need more money to cut the time it takes to get from point a to z.

Preface

It's all about creating your fiefdom; I've seen it on School Boards, in the DoD and Corporate America. Everyone wants to be the man at the top; no one wants to be the guy in the field doing the grunt work. They take the praise and bonuses when everything is done right and dole out the punishment when things go wrong. So when a politician tells you we need to raise taxes to do X, think, what is he really up to and who's going to benefit, most likely not you.

Then there's political correctness, the sugar coating of things, because words can hurt some people, really words? I'm a believer in Stick and Stones, if you don't remember it, it went something like this, Sticks and stones may break my bones but WORDS will never hurt me! If words hurt then this society has not only jumped the shark, democracy itself is close to an end. Government growth unchecked will kill any democracy faster than a plague or pestilence. When people become afraid to express themselves, because they may hurt someone, it stifles ideas, it reduces opportunities and in the end we all lose.

Preface

The sole purpose of this book is to get you to think, to open your mind, to look around and literally to stop, pause smell the roses. Look around at you current life, has the political system benefited you? Are you paying more taxes and complaining more about politicians than you have in the past? Are you sick and tired of them pandering to the special interests so they bankroll them in the next election. Then read this book, stand with me and say HELL NO! NO More! Political correctness has allowed them to pull the wool over our eyes, everything is sugar coated, so it doesn't offend anyone. How do you defend against something if you don't know what it is? Think for yourself, get away from the herd mentality, call things what they are, we don't need sentences or stereotypes to describe things, call it what it is, don't sugar coat it with political correctness, if we continue to do that, democracy is doomed to fail.

Immigration

Immigration

We are a nation of immigrants that is a fact; however we are also a nation of laws. Those laws no matter how archaic to some are there to guide the overall policy. This does not mean that anyone seeking to immigrate to the United States has a right to. You can apply and be rejected for any number of reasons, and that's good. Open border advocates see it as a bad thing; they believe anyone should be able to entry the country at any time. I'd agree if we lived in a utopian society, we don't. There is a constant threat of terrorism, drug smuggling, sex trafficking and a host of other issues with open borders. Not knowing who is in your country can not only increase the crime rate, it will increase a host of costs associated with living in that country. That said the only people who have a right to be in the United States are those who are here legally, whether by citizenship, green card or some other form of government sponsored status. In all cases those without this type of status are here illegally, now that's only a civil offense, you would think in a time where a nations security is paramount, it would be a criminal offense, but as you'll see the politicians like it this way. They see Illegal's as future voters, not as potential problems and a burden on the taxpayer. So let's get down to it, they keep promising immigration reform, and the only thing we get is amnesty so I'm going provide a common sense approach to the policy.

Immigration

The Current immigration problems go beyond Illegal Immigrants or visa expirations, it includes a whole host of items that a Politician will never speak to directly. They'll always say the system is broke, but they never seem to fix it in a way to benefit the citizens of our great country. People come here get their green cards and wait years before they can become citizens, yet each time immigration reform is promised they always let the Illegal's, jump in line ahead of those who've done the hard work. Notice I'm not calling them undocumented aliens, or anything else for that matter. If you come here without documentation, overstay a visa, slip across the border, either north or south, you are in this country as an ILLEGAL, it's that simple.

I'm not saying that all illegal immigrants are criminals. Most are here to provide for a family back home, now would I begrudge that? Yes, they're not paying income taxes and using resources meant for those here legally. They tie up the immigration court system, get deported and return. So is there a better way of dealing with this than the current one? You bet, and it's not amnesty.

Unlike many I have a problem with allowing illegal's to jump ahead in line with amnesty, for one thing who says they've been here for a certain amount of time? How does one prove one has been in a country for any number of years, when they are not there legally? More importantly if they do have this information, declaring when they arrived, why would you take that as a valid document? If they've broken the law by being here illegally, who says the documentation they provided isn't fake.

Immigration

In fairness to those who follow the rules, you cannot let those who are here in any illegal fashion jump ahead in line. If you've come here, established roots and applied for a green card, why should someone who is literally working in the shadows get a chance to jump the line? Are we a Nation of rules and laws or just a Nation of well, if you did this then, we can overlook that.

The arguments abound on this topic of amnesty, every reason is given from they pay taxes to they contribute to society. Yet all I see is my Taxes going up to fund schools that routinely fail the children they teach. I see people gaining benefits that our own citizens cannot get until a certain age, because of their legal status. I see society paying for a group of people, who should be either paying for themselves or not be here at all. So let me break down the areas of Immigration that are the easiest to fix, I'll put them in an order that makes sense and you can decide if you agree. If not that's fine we all have a right to our own opinions, an perhaps one day politicians will actually follow through fixing the immigration system.

Immigration
14th Amendment

So how did we get to birthright citizenship? If you're born in the United States to citizens of the country it a no brainier right, you're a citizen.   So how do we let people who come here on visas, overstay visitation or come here illegally and have a child and that child obtains instant citizenship? It's simple, we allowed the politicians to bastardize the fourteenth amendment and create birth right citizenship. The fourteenth amendment was established to allow the freed slaves at the time to become citizens of the United States, provide equal protection, due process and property rights to them. It was never intended to allow people to come to the country, have a baby and then in turn get the child get the benefits of citizenship. It's just another case of politicians doing what's in their best interests, and not the interests of the people they're suppose to be serving, the citizens of the United States. The text is so open borders centric you wonder why no one stood up back then and said "hey wait"; shouldn't we be wondering about x.

This is an excerpt from the fourteenth amendment "All persons born or naturalized in the United States and subject to the jurisdiction thereof, are citizens of the United States". Talk about an open invitation, but back in the eighteen hundreds things were simpler, they weren't dealing with terrorism like we have today, no drug epidemic, and taxation, while there was some it was no near prevalent as it is today.

How do we fix it? We cannot retroactively remove that citizenship without an outcry.   Why do we allow people to come here have a child and stay since they're child is now considered a citizen.

Immigration
14th Amendment

Why has no one challenged it? You would think since the Supreme Court granted an free education to illegal's back in the 1980's, someone would have filed in the courts, especially with the cost of education growing by leaps and bounds every year. Yet no one has, is it because they have to show standing? I believe we all have standing in this case so why do we let it continue? Simple, we vote for the same politicians time after time, who claim they'll fix it, and once they're back in office they conveniently forget, until re-election time.

We're also to blame, we all have compassion for our fellow man, no matter where they come from, and that's not a bad thing. Having compassion is what created the United States, problem is our compassion has become complacency, and it's used against us time and time again for the benefit of others. We lost the idea of merit being a consideration for being granting citizenship. That's the way it was years ago, you had to have a job and be able to support yourself and family or you would not be admitted. So we need to get back to that, there's nothing wrong with requiring people to be able to support themselves prior to gaining entry.

We need to stop and look at the rest of the world and what it's becoming. When you do, don't look at it through the rose colored glasses of the politicians, special interests or the media, they're all in it for themselves, votes and viewers. You need to look at it for yourself, ask the basic questions, who, what when where and why, then decide.

Immigration
14th Amendment

The amendment is so out of date with the issues of today it needs to updated or superseded with a new immigration law, so unless one or both parents of the child are citizens, the child should not be considered a citizen. If both parents were born outside the country and they do not have citizenship themselves, no matter how they entered the country, there child should not be considered a citizen; it's not fair to those born here legally and as a country we can no longer afford it.

So we fix the amendment, closing the loophole politicians have used to allow people to come here have a child and claim that child is a citizen, by making it very specific. Just because you're born in a place doesn't mean you have a right to remain there. The fix would be simple; A child born in the United States, where neither parent was or is a citizen, would be entitle to decide if they wish to apply for full citizenship on their twenty-first birthday. They do not get to remain in the United States, and must return with their parents to the country of their parents birth, but can return as a citizen once they reach the age of twenty-one, after petitioning the United States for said citizenship.

Easy fix, will politicians do it? Probably not, but it's an easy common sense fix to a problem years in the making.

Immigration
Illegal Immigrants

Illegal Immigrants, yes I said it, there not undocumented immigrants there not here legally, and as such are Illegal Immigrants.   When people hear this, they go right to your biased, there more than just Mexican nationals here illegally. You're correct; there are many different nationalities, the Irish, Italians, Germans, Chinese, Indian, Canadians and so on. So why is the focus on one group out of dozens that come in illegally?   Simple, Latinos make up a large percentage of the population, growing at a much higher rate than others, as such politicians see them as a votes, not as citizens, not as a group to work with, but as a group to pander to.

I still find it amazing that if you're here illegally you can only be changed with a misdemeanor crime. Imagine that, you can take resources you don't contribute to, take benefits you're not entitled to and if you're caught, it's a slap on the wrist. That's the first item that needs to be fixed as far as immigration goes. We need to elevate the punishment to fit the crime.

So I'd propose that the crime of illegal immigration, to include visa expirations, illegal border crossing, overstaying visitation, and any other form of undocumented stay or illegal non-citizen status be raised to a Class A level 1 Felony.

Immigration
Illegal Immigrants

It should be a crime punishable by immediate deportation to ones country of origin or birth, no appeals process, if you're not a citizen, the appeals process should not apply. Subsequently, a fine of a minimum of 250,000 US dollars and all transportation costs will to be billed and payment expected form the country of origin. Failure of that country to pay would result in the deduction of that amount per national from any type of aid promised to said country. So effectively if you're country is getting a subsidy form the US in the form of foreign aid, it gets reduced for each instance above.

No wall, no need, walls would require maintenance, a deep foundation, five to ten feet down, rebar, concrete, and anti-tunnel technologies that can detect vibrations down fifty, one hundred, two hundred or more feet. They can be climbed, so you'd need razor wire on top, then litigation starts when someone climbs the wall and gets a cut, I can see the lawyers lining up for at action. It also interferes with the environment; animals move back and forth, they breed in certain locations so the very idea of a wall invokes litigation, environment review and the courts. So how do we deal with it? There are a number of ways, from more Border patrols to robotics and drones. The border can and must be secured, in an era where terrorism is running rampant; we need to know who is coming in. Open borders worked a hundred or so years ago, they will not today.

Immigration
Illegal Immigrants

Cities play a big part in illegal immigration as well, by not providing support to the federal government and in essence perpetuating the status quo, thus providing material support to a known foreign entity living illegally on US soil. As such and to prevent these "Sanctuary Cities" from continuing this activity, those States found to contain or harbor Sanctuary Cities, will lose all Federal Funding. This includes but is not limited to, education, transportation, police, fire and any supplemental funding for health care would be suspended until the State and for mentioned City in question can prove they are not harboring known foreign nationals, also known as illegal immigrants.

How do we validate that? It's complex but not undoable. The City and State would need to provide the total number of residents, and the place of birth, no names or addresses. School records would also need to be provided, no names or addresses just total number of students, class size, and alike along with birth and any related court records.   You'd be amazed at what simple data like this can tell you about a City and its inhabitance.

Should the number not match federal data such as social security numbers for that give area, the penalties would begin, starting at twenty five percent of total federal funding including police, fire, transportation, roads and rails, and exponentially grow.

Immigration
Illegal Immigrants

This information would be required to be submitted once every six months, upon review penalties would be assessed increasing twenty five percent per six month cycle up to one hundred percent of funding, or be reduced depending on the status. This would include work in progress at the time of the infraction, and may result in cost over runs for the State or localities which would not be reimbursable. It would put the costs on the back of local taxpayers, and given time these sanctuary cities will no longer exist. The people would make the political changes necessary to insure these cities would change. Make people pay the cost associated with the belief and in time the pocket book wins.

The church plays a role in this as well, they can provide sanctuary for any number of reasons as such should any place of worship be found harboring illegal immigrants, the tax exempt status they enjoy should no longer apply. However this is only in the case of illegals. There are other reasons to seek sanctuary in a place of worship, those would not be impacted by the above, however once the tax exemption is lifted it cannot be regained. It also would apply to all places of worship associated, so for example if it was a Catholic church in New Jersey, all Catholic churches across the country would lose any federal exemption. Too harsh? Again you're basically harboring a person who has no legal standing to be in the country and violating the legal statues on immigration. Hence you are and accomplice to the violation of law. Currently illegal immigration is a civil offense, this above would apply once the law changed making illegal immigration a felony.

Immigration
Illegal Immigrants

In addition to the loss of funding since the Federal immigration code spells out specific penalties, for harboring illegals.   One part specifically in U.S. immigration Code › Title 8 › Chapter 12 › Subchapter II › Part VIII › § 1324, in sub section (iii) knowing or in reckless disregard of the fact that an alien has come to, entered, or remains in the United States in violation of law, conceals, harbors, or shields from detection, or attempts to conceal, harbor, or shield from detection, such alien in any place, including any building or any means of transportation;

The penalties allowable currently range from a fine to up to twenty years in prison, but who really gets fined, too few in my view. So if politicians want to make their cities sanctuary cities, I propose that for each vote in favor and/or Mayoral or Governor signature, each person involved with the approval, hence voting yes, from Politicians to lawyers and even Judges be given the maximum of 20 years no chance of parole, no fine, just a standard sentence for creating a safe harbor for foreign nationals who are in the country illegally. That being anything from over staying a visa, illegal border crossing, north or south, visa or visitation overstays. The change in law should also apply to persons who support the eluding of persons slated for ICE deportation. It would gain the same status as if you harbored a criminal from prosecution.

Immigration
Illegal Immigrants

On the flip side we have companies who hire illegal's to do work and pay them under the table. The jobs range from farming, landscaping and construction to technical jobs, resulting in lower wages for Americans. As such the I9 program was created to try and vet out illegals from those authorized to live in and work in the United States. If you were to knowingly hire an Illegal to do work for you and you got caught, the initial penalty is five hundred and thirty nine dollars for each violation.   If you're caught doing it for the third time or more the fine increases to twenty one thousand five hundred and sixty three dollars. Now if you're paying someone under the table at five to ten dollars an hour and you get hit with the larger fine, you'd probably think twice before doing it again. So I propose the punishment fit the crime.

If you as an employer knowingly hire an illegal alien to work for your company, no matter who authorized it, the minimum fine should be one hundred thousand dollars per violation. So if you have ten illegal's working for you, that's a million dollars and so on. That portion of the fine would go to the federal government. The State in which you reside would also be entitled to a penalty of seventy five thousand dollars per infraction. So again ten illegal's working for your company if caught would result in a fine of seven hundred and fifty thousand dollars on top of the Federal penalty.

Immigration
Illegal Immigrants

This would result in a total cost to the business of one million seven hundred and fifty thousand dollars. The Federal government and State would also have a right to place this penalty on a company for a maximum of five years. Now should a second violation be found that could be an added penalty for a five year period on top of the current penalty, when you impact the finances of a person or company, you get their attention very quickly.

If these changes were enacted and enforced, you'd see illegal immigration almost vanish. It would never go completely away, the Supreme Court took care of that by allowing illegal's to attend public schools in the United States.   While it makes sense if there here legally, it does not if they're illegal, they are breaking what is currently a civil law, that needs to be changed to a class one felony. Other changes should include a one language policy, if you need something translated from English to any number of other languages, you should bear the burden not government. If you need in school support, and you're legal, it should be offered, in an English immersion program, not English as a second language. All documentation should be published in English, reducing the burden on taxpayers, and placing it where it belongs on the person needing the translation.

Immigration
Illegal Immigrants

Immigration changes aren't meant to be heartless, they're meant to put the citizens of this country first, and the rest of the world second. What wrong with putting ourselves first? The rest of the world does it, they expect the Americans to be the first to defend them when conflict arises, so we need to start putting ourselves first. It's nice to be nice, but when it has a negative impact, nice is no longer nice.

Immigration
Refugees

If a country's government falls apart how do you validate that a person is from said country, let alone if there a criminal or not, you simply cannot. Refugees come to America for a number of reasons, political, religious and so on. So it begs the question, outside of political or religious persecution why would you accept refugees?   In the case of a civil war, do you accept refugees even though the government can neither confirm nor deny the person or persons lived, were born in or inhabited the country in question? It's nice to be nice and help others I get that, but today when so much is at risk due to terrorism and ideological beliefs, why take the chance.

In the US we have a homeless problem, families, veterans, people with multitudes of problems living on the streets and we take in refugees. We have a department in the federal government that is specifically designed to find affordable housing for refugees. Yet we have no such department for US Citizens, sure there's HUD, but it boggles the mind that we continue to help the rest of the world before we help ourselves. In this case we give subsidized sometimes free housing to people who are not citizens, and leave the citizens to pay for themselves.   The government budget for this program was over one billion dollars in 2012. You're tax dollars at work, even with the fee collection for each individual, if it's not waived, it just another way to support everyone else at the expense of the citizens of the United States.

Immigration
Refugees

So how do we fix it? We want to help, were not a nation of immigrants by accident, we help others, but we need to start making fundamental changes or this country is in big trouble. We start by saying NO, everyone wants to come to the US, it's the land of milk and honey, that is until you get here and get your tax bill, but I digress. If people want to come here, they should have to be able to provide for themselves, if they cannot, or a sponsor cannot financially, they should not be allowed into the country, let alone be given benefits and support our citizens and veterans can't get. No immigrant or refugee should be entitled to any benefit until they obtain some form of citizenship status. We had a merit based system before and we need it again.

We should not discriminate based on financial status, but we have our own problems we need to tackle, health care, homelessness, poverty and education to name a few. We should be focusing our resources on those endeavors and stop being the nice guy of the world. The billon plus dollars spent here would go a long way to help American citizens get back on their feet, especially veterans and homeless. So why do we spend it on people who want to flee their own country?

Immigration
Refugees

This refugee and immigration program is not just about people who are persecuted at home, it's also for entrepreneurs. Yes there is a specific fee listed on and rules as to what percentage of a company you must own to qualify. So we're basically selling citizenship and green cards to those who can afford them. Why? We put down our own people, the people who actually pay taxes to support government and open the doors to everyone else.

Refugees are a problem across the world, not just for the United States, but the rest of the world is not our problem. Our problem is here, on our own soil, selling access and damming the citizens of this country to second tier status. I'm not saying to lock the borders, what I am saying is limit those who can enter, require some basic financial stability on their part and require them to learn English, if they don't already speak it. We required it in the past, so why not go back to a standard that worked for so many years? It's common sense unless you're a politician.

Immigration
Guest Worker Program

In some shape or form we do need to develop a guest worker program, where you allow a certain number or people into a country to work, and after a period of time they go home. You would think with today's technology a system like this would be easy to setup and administrate. You'd be right except, it depends on people being honest and trustworthily. I'm not saying all of those taking advantage wouldn't be, what I am saying is don't bet against the human condition. You may have people sign affidavits staying they'll go back home after said number of days but how do you enforce it?

One way would be to provide GPS bracelets that would have to be worn while working in the US. Knowing how litigious our society is, how long do you think it would take before the ACLU, or some other group filed suit against monitoring as part of the program? I'd give it maybe three months and we'd be back to no monitoring, no tracking, back to your word is your bond. Now I don't know about you, but I was brought up to believe that. You make a promise you keep it to the best of your ability. What I'm not sure about is the rest of the world's interpretation of that.

Another method would be to withhold fifty or seventy five percent of earnings for each guest worker. If they fail to report in, they forfeit the money. While this would provide some level of compensation to the government, the simple fact is if someone wants to stay bad enough no amount of money to be forfeited will impact there disappearing into the shadows.

Immigration
Guest Worker Program

We'd just be creating a new class of illegal that started as a guest worker and overstayed, similar to an expired visa.

The only true way to implement this program is to start it out small and phase it in over time. Background checks would need to be run on each person applying for a position in the guest worker program. Fingerprints would have to be taken; all information including job location and place of residence along with valid photo identification would be stored in a centralized database, accessible to the FBI, Homeland Security and local police. Government sponsorship of each and every person applying for a guest worker permit in the United States is required.

Each government would have to account for their citizens at the start and the end of the program. As part of the program, governments will put aside two hundred and fifty thousand dollars per applicant, in a fund dedicated to the tracking of guest workers. Should a person not return to their home country, the government sponsoring said guest worker would automatically forfeit the dedicated monies to the United States Treasury along with any outstanding salary the person had yet to collect. The account and monies included would be administrated by the Department of Homeland Security, with all funds required prior to the person or persons entering the program.

Immigration
Guest Worker Program

Should a person participating in the program commit a crime while in the United States, the money would be forfeit and the person returned to their country of origin or sponsoring country. This would be true in any criminal case from a misdemeanor crime or felony. Other crimes such as murder, rape or other serious offences would result in imprisonment in the Unites States.

In the case of a more serious offense the country sponsoring the person convicted of said crime would also be liable for all fees associated with the incarceration of said person, that being room, board, medical, clothing, legal fees and alike. This would not be a onetime thing it's to be paid from the start of the legal proceedings to the inmate's day of release and subsequent deportation. Should a country refuse to pay, there are other legal remedies that would be build into the contacts, starting with a fine, plus the supporting dollars for their citizen, to expulsion of all guest workers from that particular country and confiscation of all monies paid, except for the wages paid to date for those workers. If that occurred said country would not be allowed to participate in the program for a set period, not to be less than two or more than five years.

Immigration
Path to Citizenship

In the current immigration laws, there is no clearly defined way for an Illegal immigrant to move forward and get on the right side of the law, thus becoming a citizen of the United States.   There are a lot of different ways this could be done, the politicians favorite Amnesty, just grant them the right that they took full advantage of in the first place.   That only benefits the politicians not the citizens of this great country and I for one am sick of the politicians benefiting while the citizens of this country get taxed to death to support them.

In order to determine the path, we'd need some information from the Illegal. Names as well as assumed names, place of residence, county of origin and any documentation as to citizenship from said country of origin as a start. Hospital records, birth records for children, school records, based on that information you can then determine how long said person and/or family has been living in the United States illegally. It's a start, not fool proof by any means but a start to get an idea of when a person came here. You could also through in landlord sworn statements, or other physical information that could help determine a hard date.

Once the date is established, the person applying for citizenship would then need to provide documentation on past work. If they do not have any documentation and have been a day laborer, paid under the table in a restaurant or any business, if they owned their own business, all records of income along with employer identification where applicable, must be submitted as part of the application.

Immigration
Path to Citizenship

This information would show how much if any taxes in the form of Income, Social Security, Property or other taxes they've paid to the benefit of society.

So far we're doing a background check, historical work up, job history and tax payments in any form other than sales tax. Sales tax, is limited in use, it does not offset income or property taxes to support the State or schools. So the sales tax argument when most people say "Illegal's pay Taxes" fails here and is not included as part of the overall documentation required to start the process. A standard FBI background check for a United States citizen, takes up to six months to complete.   Using that as a baseline the initial timeframe for the background checks to complete would be at least one year from the start of the application. It's not going to be a quick process and must include not only a background check, but criminal as well as civil investigations as well.

During this process the person applying must maintain their residence and check in at least once every eight to ten weeks to get a status. During this time they would have a provisional status, guest worker, and be allowed to work legally. Once the process is complete and all data can be vetted, the person will be contacted for a face to face interview. In the case of families, the entire family must attend the interview. This is required to review all the documentation submitted along with what the background check found.

Immigration
Path to Citizenship

It will be the person's only chance to refute any information related to them, that they believe is incorrect. Failure to appear at this interview will result in nullification of all documentation submitted, along with an arrest warrant, and subsequent deportation to said country of origin. Why so tough?

If you start the process you have to finish it, even if there is information that could invalidate your application such as criminal history, it would be better to discuss what happened when and how, then to not show up.

There needs to be some repercussions for wasting taxpayer money and time, if you're not planning on completing the process simply don't start it in the first place.   Once the person completes the Face to Face interview and signs off on the discussion, two things can happen, one further information may be required based on the newly discovered information, should that be required, the same steps noted above along with maintaining you're current residence and checking in eight to ten weeks for status.

Secondly if no further information is needed, the interviewer can then move the application forward to the office of Homeland Security. As part of this process, the person would need to pay an application fee based on prior earnings. This fee could be spread out over time in a payment plan, or a garnisheeing agreement for future earnings. Payments would be required by a specific date; late payments as with anything else would result in penalties and interest.

Immigration
Path to Citizenship

As with anything it will take time from the start of the process to the end point. The expectation is that this kind of program would take on average two to five years before citizenship   could be granted. That could be cut down, through military service or initiatives that could shave time off the process. In order to fully qualify all payments and taxes required must be paid in full prior to the granting of full citizenship.

Immigration
H1B Programs

The H1B program was designed initially to bring in "Highly Qualified" Foreign workers in the areas of Math and Science. It's now used as a tool of diversification, yes companies now bring in workers from overseas and it now goes well beyond Information Technology.   In some companies other HxB programs cover janitors up and through management positions. Why? Well when congress wrote this little ditty of a law, they set a salary of just over sixty thousand dollars for an H1B worker in the Information Technology field.   At the time that was the average IT salary, what they didn't do was link it any way to inflation, so that standard salary has not changed in twenty or so years. Today the average Information Technology salary is upwards of one hundred to one hundred and twenty thousand, so in effect companies can outsource and American job and get a two for one deal.

Unlike some people I don't blame the H1B Visa holder, I blame the grantor. If congress revised this law in any way it would cost the companies, grantors of the H1B's hundreds of millions of dollars to keep that staff. In a way were allowing the politicians and corporations to give away good paying American jobs, by not voting them out of office.   So if these people are so highly qualified and some are, I propose the following to fix this program and put the American worker first.

If they are "Highly Qualified" and you cannot find an American as qualified, something I've doubted from the start, but that's just my experience.

Immigration
H1B Programs

Then they should be highly compensated, something the current law does not do. Under the program currently the salary is set at sixty thousand dollars, a good starting salary but nowhere near the current average Information Technology salary.   So if they are so highly qualified and sought after they should be paid more, for starters let's double the current H1B minimum salary and insure all H1B workers receive the increase as soon as the law is passed. That increase would be retroactive to their start date, so if they've been in a position for five years, with their H1B status, they'd be owed some serious back pay.

The purpose of this is twofold; it will insulate the American worker from foreign competition based on wage and force companies to use the law as its intended. As it stands there are companies that are exploiting the program for everything from reducing costs, to workforce diversification. Diversity is a good thing don't get me wrong, having multiple perspectives from different backgrounds on a problem, can result in better solutions, however diversity for the bottom line is not a good thing. That results in less diversity over time as cost cutting forces less diversity.

Immigration
H1B Programs

In addition to the salary, corporation should be required to pay higher fees for these workers. Currently the fee structure starts at three hundred twenty five dollars with an additional seven hundred and fifty dollars fee if you have one to twenty five employees or one thousand five hundred dollars if you have more than twenty six full time employees. These fees are based on each application, so if these people so highly qualified, these fees should be increased as well.

Each company is different and as such has different levels of staffing or full time employees, if you have less than twenty five, you should be paying five thousand dollars per applicant to be compliant with the American Competitiveness and Workforce Improvement Act of 1998 (ACWIA). While companies with more than twenty five full time employees should be paying double that or ten thousand dollars per applicant.

These fees should then be indexed to not inflation but unemployment. If unemployment is low, then the fees only increase at five percent a year. If unemployment is high say greater than five percent or the total number of Americans currently in the labor participation rate falls below sixty two percent whichever is higher, the fees associated with these programs double. Once employment reaches the number set or exceeds the labor participation rate, the fees stabilize and grow from this point at the five percent rate.

Immigration
H1B Programs

If companies really need labor from outside the United States it should be more expensive for them to get it. They should be hiring from the internal market first and only after they cannot train and employee for the position be allowed to bring in an H1B or Highly Qualified person. This would be allowed only after a litmus test, to prove that the current crop of employees cannot do the job duties assigned and to show the need for the "Highly Qualified" person or persons. That would not be left up to the company; they would need to submit data, reviews and a host of other information related to the employees and the position before a visa should be considered. This would be done by an outside organization that would have specific restrictions on it. Those restrictions would include that lobbyists, corporate benefactors, members of boards of directors, politicians, political family members or any current or former government employees cannot work for or be associated with the organization.

Each quarter every employee would have to submit to an audit with yearly background checks and have the audits publically published. The organizations decisions are required to be substantiated and every approval must be bound by reasonable doubt with the burden of proof on the applicant. That means each approval has to be able to stand up in a court, not a board room. Other restrictions and requirements including the organization having to be a private entity run by American citizens, who would be required to have security clearances and background checks to insure they are impartial.

Immigration
H1B Programs

If that organization couldn't be stood up or until it is and we really wanted to be fair to the American worker who's impacted by this outsourcing, we'd apply an additional corporate tax, to be no less than twenty five percent of the gross earnings of each H1B hire. So at tax time, if you have ten people with this status, you'd pay twenty five percent of their combined salaries, so if it's still at sixty thousand dollars per hire, then the total applicable to this tax would be six hundred thousand dollars. Twenty five percent of which would be a tax of one hundred and fifty thousand dollars, no deductions. That money would be designated for a retraining program for outsourced employees. It would have to be carried as a separate expense on all accounting forms and listed as a separate item in both quarterly and annual reports. There is no deduction against this tax as it is for the benefit of the American worker as such as the pay increases for your H1B worker would increase this tax.

Would this impact the bottom line of every company who uses the program? Yes. Will it impact their share price, and be a burden or benefit to the share holders? Only time would tell, but implemented as I have stated above, you'd see a lot less of it, which would benefit the American people, not just the corporations and shareholders.

Politicians

Politicians

What's the difference between a Politician and a Con Man? Growing up this was a topic of conversation at times. The answer is simple, the difference is politicians, speak in tongs not lies. Not a different language, but the language of politics. Listen when they're asked questions, you never get a direct answer do you? If they do answer a direct question, you should realize two things, one they have support for whatever the idea is under discussion and you're not going to derail it. Two prepared to pay more in taxes to fund it even if it only benefits two people as long a politician see's benefit in it for themselves; the good of the few will always outweigh the good of the many.

That idea they have, no matter how small or well meaning will eventually evolve into a boondoggle long after this person is gone from office. It's inevitable, like night and day.   The law of unintended consequences follows politics like bees to honey.   The intention for what it's worth is good, they just can't see beyond reelection and therefore no due diligence is done to look into the long term ramifications. We have departments at the State and Federal level that are duplicative; politicians know that yet instead of cutting costs, were the credit card if you need proof, when's the last time you got to approve spending any money at any level of government? Never is the correct answer, so we end up with twenty trillion of debt and climbing. If this where you or I, we would cut costs, cut out a movie or dinner out, reduce our spending to lower debt, they do the exact opposite, they raise the debt ceiling.

Politicians

Imagine if you could do that, call the bank and say I want to increase my credit limits to match my spending habits. Oh yea and I'll be paying the bear minimums for the foreseeable future. Do you think the bank or banks would go for it? Even if you had millions in the bank they'd laugh at you, call you crazy and a bunch of other names once they hang up. How do we fix this? A balanced budget amendment would be a good start, maybe go back on the gold standard and stop the Federal Reserve from printing money. All these ideas and a multitude of others will get nowhere until we the people stop electing the same politicians over and over. Think for a minute, they're supposed to work for us, right? So why do we extend their careers when they do nothing to benefit us, the citizens of this country?

Growing up in New Jersey it still amazing to me that the same politicians that allowed the introduction of the Property tax and subsequently the Income tax still get reelected year after year. But then they blame the Supreme Court, which constitutionally, isn't allowed to define the way dollars are spent, but still does. The State Supreme Court has never shied away from costing taxpayer's money, which is a constitutional violation, yet the assembly where all spending is to originate from in this State does nothing, to whose benefit? People blindly re-elect the same people time after time and expect things to change. Those people follow the clearest definition of insanity, doing the same things over and over expecting a different outcome.

Politicians

The only changes I've seen are costs housing costs, food, necessities, and transportation etc. going through the roof. They'll tell you it because New Jersey is the most densely populated State, so things cost more, yet there afraid of balancing those costs. Case in point, NJ Transit, if the riders were not subsidized, the system would fail, oh and that subsidy comes from the gas tax, another fund they robed blind. So how do you justify using the gas tax to fund this, simple the general fund. In NJ like in DC, there are no constitutionally defined funds, where money collect must go by law. It all goes into a general fund, where is squandered on pet project, meaningless laws and repetitive bills that have no chance in passing.

Case in Point the Affordable Care Act, Republicans tried forty or more times to repeal it. Did they really believe Obama would sign it? No, they don't have a veto proof majority so why bother, its political grandstanding and a waste of tax dollars. They do it all the time, and no one holds the politician accountable. They exempt themselves from legislation, like the Affordable Care Act and no one bats an eye. Did you know up until a few years ago insider trading was legal for them? Yup one more for the elitist's while if you or I do it, well there's jail time and fines, but we don't matter we only elect them and pay the bills.

Politicians

When Wall Street got the billions in bailout funds, we the people were getting pink slips. The rich get richer, poor get poorer and the middle class get to pay for it all. My definition of middle class does not match the Democrat or Republican one. So let start there, the middle class in some States is defined as someone making up to seventy five thousand dollars per year, not bad, until you look at the tax burdens. Middle class to me depends on a number of factors; family size, having 8 children on that 75k salary would put you at the poverty level in the north east.   That same amount in the south with the same number of children can put you in a very different situation. So for me the middle class or the very idea of it depends on where you live, that's common sense, something that is severely lacking these days in a multitude of areas. Yet politicians local and at the federal level talk about us in general, lumping people in and pulling others out... Ask yourself, if there always looking to help the middle class, why is it they never do? We pay the majority of taxes or at least it seems that way, take the brunt of programs that allow good paying jobs to be shipped overseas or outsourced at home, and yet keep electing the same schmucks year after year.

Remember the Occupy Wall Street crowd? Protesting the one percent, the millionaires and billionaires and those who've been very successful? One thing they overlooked in all that protesting was who else is part is of that one to two percent. They had them as guest speakers and they sat with them, gave them ideas that went nowhere. The politicians, you have members of congress, former presidents who join or participate in these movements, all for show all for votes.

Politicians

They don't care about what you're protesting, its TV time, face time for them, they all do the same thing so you have to wonder, why we keep blindly following the same two parties.

The idea that it's not my guy its yours has created a self fulfilling prophecy, they get reelected and screw us over every election cycle until they decide not to run, they get indicted, and walk away on oh it was done out of friendship, they're protected, leverage their positions and if we did it, well there's jail time. They get cushy jobs afterwards in some other area of government or move into the private sector, we'd be on unemployment. Keep in mind when a politician moves into a private sector job, it not like you or I, oh no they get the corner office with the views; you get the cube near the kitchen.

They get bonuses, six to seven figure salaries as a start, you get to do the work then when your salary starts to rise you get to train your replacement. If you're lucky, you find another job and the cycle starts again. I've seen it over and over where once you're making good money I'm not talking one hundred and fifty thousand plus, you just start to break may be one hundred thousand or start getting close to it if you're lucky then in IT especially the outsourcing begins. Is it justifiable, maybe if you're of the mindset that the company comes before country that stock holders come before ethics, that executives do more for the business than someone in the trenches, doing the day to day work that makes the company money.

Politicians

Corporations have a responsibility to the citizens in the country where it was established, not to the rest of the world. One thing to remember is a Corporation once founded is considered a legal person and has many of the same rights and responsibilities as natural persons. As such they are citizens of their country of origin, and have in my summation responsibilities to that country first and foremost. Yet the politicians allow them to through programs and provide incentives to move jobs overseas or import workers when they claim they can't find qualified Americans. So who's at fault for allowing this? Is it the Corporation, Its stock holders, Unions, all of the above? Yes in a way, we are all part of these organizations, and pay in one way or another, each one in turn supporting the politicians in one way or another.

Those politicians benefit from their benefactors, who in turn benefit from the politician. So where do we stand? We get to vote for the politicians, they support, and we blindly go and vote like sheep, not taking the time to even look at a voting record, to see how bad they've screwed us in the past. Not looking outside the political party we've been voting for years because one year they're going to do what we want, my dad told me so, or my grandfather... We've always been democrats I can't vote republican, we've always been republicans I can't vote for a democrat and the cycle of insanity continues, and we the people get what we deserve.

Politicians

Take the H1B visa program; it was originally designed to bring highly educated foreigners to staff positions in situations where a qualified American candidate couldn't be found. That of course was subjective and now a day's its use to bring in people to keep costs down.   Are they qualified? According to the corporations they are, ask some of them about their function and they can't answer, mostly because they don't know, they're kept in the dark like the rest of us. I'm not putting them down far from it; I've seen firsthand how hard these people work for the wages paid and hours they put in. There definitely on par in most cases with their American counterpart, well except for that salary.

Companies now are using the H1B program in the name of diversifying the work force. Really we need to import diversity with the number of Americans both unemployed and out of the labor markets, those who have just given up. It's Just another unintended consequence of a law that is being interpreted way too broadly, benefiting the corporations while the tax payers get soaked. So politicians want to help the middle class, they want everyone to go to college. How do you justify spending two hundred thousand dollars or more on a computer science, engineering or other high tech degrees, when the job will be shipped overseas as soon as a corporate bean counter decides you're making too much?

Politicians

That executive bean counter doesn't have to worry about being outsourced, they have the golden parachutes, and buddies in the boardroom to watch their backs. They get bonuses in the millions of dollars for cutting costs, what do you get? Depending on the company two weeks for every year in severance, that won't get you too far now a days. What do the politicians get? They get more money for the next election cycle, does unemployment concern them? In my option no, if it did then anyone not working would be counted as unemployed and we'd have a true number, not the farcical number of today's unemployment numbers. The government gives one number then revises it up, down left then right, are they real numbers, one hopes so but it's the government, so do we really know?

Politicians will complain that corporations make way too much money. That a CEO is over payed tens if not hundreds of times in relation to the lowest paid worker. They'll say the minimum wage is too low. Yet that same politician will turn around and take thousands if not millions of dollars from those corporations come election time. Politicians have Political Action Committees with billions of dollars backing them, where does that money come from corporations, billionaires, millionaires, and unions, where do they get the money? In a lot of cases the middle class, one corporation I worked for asked annually for PAC contributions. That company I will not name, however its CEO controls one of the largest PACs in D.C. and we wonder why things just keep getting more expensive and further out of reach. We effectively keep doing it to ourselves.

Politicians

We keep doing the same things over and over expecting a different result, because this guy I'm voting for said this... Ask yourself, they said something that caught you interest, but did it really answer the question that was asked at the time? Or was it a smokescreen as usual.

When it comes to wages, I do agree in the current environment all wages not just the minimum are too low. People haven't seen a real raise in years, you're lucky to see two percent at most companies one percent at others and in some nothing at all for years, even with them making record profits. So what's the answer? Stop pushing good paying jobs overseas and start penalizing companies who do. Will politicians do it? That would benefit the middle class, but they benefit from the system as is, campaign contributions trump common sense.

Just look at the way unemployment is measured, you need to be "Actively Looking" to be counted, that allows the politicians to sugar coat the numbers to match what they want you to think. Back in the nineteen seventies participation in the work force was sixty three percent. That's factored on the total number of people sixteen and over who could be working versus total population. We had a much higher participation rate in the late nineteen nineties and early two thousands from nineteen ninety seven to two thousand and one total labor participation was on average sixty seven percent, today its down to just sixty two point nine percent. These numbers are from the Bureau of Labor Statistics (http://data.bls.gov/pdq/SurveyOutputServlet).

Politicians

They're updated monthly and you can see for yourself.

If you were to count all the people able but not looking for work, unemployment would be over 9%. That's counting everyone sixteen and over that would like to work but has not looked for a job or has not gotten back into the job market.

Let's not get stuck on the numbers, look at it this way, as of August two thousand seventeen the labor participation rate as published by the Bureau of Labor Statistics stood at sixty two point nine percent. In essence, you have forty seven point one percent of the population not actively participating in the workforce. To find a lower participation rate you'd have to go back to March of nineteen seventy eight, where you'd have forty seven point two percent of the population not actively participating and unemployment at six point seven percent. If you want the real numbers you have to dig in and look for them, otherwise you get the much lower unemployment number, which doesn't tell the whole economic story.   It's all about controlling the message.

Have you noticed a Politician will from time to time whenever they want to push up the minimum wage for example, talk about it costing too much to live and people need a living wage? If they'd only look in the mirror they'd see one of the major factors in that cost. Back in the nineteen seventies you could buy a car for two thousand dollars, a very nice one for around six thousand and a starter home for between eighteen and thirty thousand dollars.

Politicians

Today the average starter home price on the east coast is close to two hundred thousand. In just over forty years housing costs have quintupled, what else happened during that time period that may have had an impact? Inflation during the latter part of the nineteen seventies was running amuck, pushing up costs.

However if you look at taxation in that time period, properly and income taxes became all the rage in a lot of States pushing up basic living costs, which in turn pushes up food, clothing and housing costs, so don't let them fool you, follow the money.

Why does it cost almost two million dollars per mile to pave a New Jersey road, while it only costs eighteen thousand in the Carolinas? Politicians will have you know New Jersey is the most densely populated State, so things cost more. This in fact it has more to do with the political climate, election cycles, regulation and any number of inflationary costs.

I use New Jersey in the book, it's my home, it's also been corrupt since before this nation formed so to me there's no surprise that just about everything costs more in New Jersey. Every swine has his head in the trough, and nothing stops them, in New Jersey there is no difference between a Republican and a Democrat. They both play the same games, allow for cities to provide tax abatements, while the rest of the State pays to support their schools.

Politicians

Then allowing those same cities to go thirty to forty or more years with our reevaluating property, is that fair no, should it be allowed? Hell no, but they allow it to pander to the base. Billions upon Billions wasted, in the schools construction corporation debacle, did anyone in New Jersey go to jail, nope, we all just went deeper in debt.

I see Property Taxes as regressive. If you believe in quality education, than everyone should be paying a fair share, and that's done via a sales or income tax, not on the backs of property owners. The equitable way would be to only raise property taxes once a property is sold, the number a municipality, City or the State puts on it is arbitrary at best and it's in their interest not yours. Just because they say the property is worth a certain amount doesn't mean that a buyer would pay that price, it's simply a gimmick for them to get your hard earned money and redistribute it around the State.

We have cities in New Jersey that are utter failures where eighty to ninety percent of the funding to support them comes from the State. We have politicians who in the nineteen seventies decided to build Casinos in Atlantic City, never fixing up the areas beyond the boardwalk, who now can't figure out why that City is failing. Yes, most of those same politicians are still running the State. In the nineteen seventies the State Supreme court and governor created the property tax and subsequent income tax system.

Politicians

The Income tax was suppose to pay back property owners for funding the education system, you can guess how that's been going, smaller and smaller amounts returned to property owners, making less and less money. Politicians in New Jersey figured out long ago, if they want something, eventually the Supreme Court will get pushed into the topic and cost the taxpayers more.

The constitution has limits and guidance just like the one at the federal level, except in New Jersey it's a piece of paper, trampled on at will by the political elitists that run the State. They simply don't care that appropriations are suppose to only come from the assembly, they simply let the court make up the rules, and they play along continually get reelected.

Another more recent example was the gas tax, they wanted to raise it twenty three cents per gallon to fix the transportation trust fund. Only after the democrats and republicans were challenged did it come out that that money was not going to the fund. It wasn't earmarked and was going like the rest of tax dollars into the general fund. Why? Pensions and benefits, light rail systems, some road work and a lot of pandering to the base for future votes. Did they even try to constitutionally guarantee the funds? Yes, they actually did, and the voters approved it. Was it a wise decision, not if you read the fine print, it allows them to borrow more money, for more projects.

Politicians

It's all in the wording and fine print when it comes to ballot questions, there's never enough real information, just enough to give you an impression in the direction they want you to vote. In New Jersey, we see tax hikes, never cuts, oh no we don't have a spending problem, we have a revenue problem.   Just like in DC, the people are seen as cash cows to be milked for every pet project, to be used as collateral, and to be on the hook when it all goes downhill.

Think about this, if you took twenty trillion dollars the current size of the national debt, in dollar bills and laid it out. Each dollar being about six inches long, with one mile being sixty three thousand six hundred and sixty inches. So for each mile you use ten thousand five hundred and sixty dollars. If you divide twenty trillion by ten thousand five hundred and sixty dollars and you end up with one trillion eight hundred ninety three billion, nine hundred and thirty nine thousand, three hundred and ninety three point ninety four miles. In essence you'd be circling the equator seven six thousand, fifty seven point twenty four times.

A better visual of that debt may be if you spent twenty dollars per second, to spend one million dollars it would take would take about five hundred and eight seven days, about a year and a half or so. To spending a billion dollars at the same rate would take about one thousand five hundred and eighty five years.

Politicians

Now take the billion and divide it into twenty trillion, spending at the same rate, it would take thirty one billion seven hundred thousand years. So you get the idea and that doesn't factor in Pensions, benefits and other ongoing costs, the real debt number is much higher than the actual debt clock. That only shows currently what the government has spent; it does not take into account future spending, on those pensions and benefits they've promised.

Same with most States, they run deficits as well and in most cases have to balance the budgets by the end of the year constitutionally. So what you see as a deficit year to year isn't the real number, if you add in the political promises, pensions, benefits, and other payouts for not using sick and vacation time, you'll see the real number. In New Jersey, they say the deficit is around thirty eight to forty billion. That's not taking pension or benefits into account, same as the national debt clock, so you know the real number is probably two to four or more times higher. After all, the taxpayer is just a credit card to support their spending.

Politicians
Liberals and Conservatives

Liberal orthodoxy implies that they know what you want better than you do, therefore, they should be able to get you to take what they are offering you. They know better, they know you want a hamburger, but they'll try to talk you into a hot dog or a salad, the salad is better for you right? So why not have that. Conservatives are a little different, taxes are too high, we need free markets, and the defense of the country is paramount.   True statements, but they'll try to sell you a pile of goods as well.

Each of these ideals are just that, ideals, yet both will sell you or I down the river to insure they get reelected. So there's something they have in common, they believe they're better than us, know better than us and can lead us down the primrose path, sad part is we let them and it's not for our betterment. We need to start to realize, we don't need them, they need us.

We live in a two party system technically or at least a two major party system; why? Because we all want to be on the side of a winner, so we don't even look at the Libertarian party, let alone any other. We let them use the media to pull us in, to make up our minds for us, they distract us from the real issues of the day, they guide us to what they want us to believe, create a fifth estate of sorts and pander so they can get reelected over and over. When did politics become not only a full time job but almost a guaranteed one?

Politicians
Liberals and Conservatives

That happened the day we stopped paying attention, we let the distractions take away from what really needs to happen. We let the media spin us into segments, then grouping and tailored news to insulate and confuse. They use the same tried and true methods from back in the late eighteen and early nineteen hundreds, it was called yellow journalism then, meant to distract or insight with little to no real factual content. The news isn't fake news it's tailored to the whims of the of the media owners, not to the actual news event in most cases.

Look at the world as it currently stands, we want democracy to spread, our ideals to be the best, yet the people who push these changes have little to no understanding of the history or culture they're trying to change. You can go country by country where democracy has started and failed countries where terrorism is spreading, where idea that one sex is smarter and has more right than the other. That's the surface, what's below?   Its part of the basic concept, a standard set of questions who, what, where, when and why, all the politician sees is me. Over the past fifty years, we've gotten it wrong, why?

Politicians
Liberals and Conservatives

Vietnam wanted to be a democracy, they didn't want communism all they wanted was the French to leave. So what did we do, of course we ignored them, and supported the French and our soldiers paid the price, thousands of American lives lost in the process, others who've never come home, there lost to history for now. So why do we continually allow politicians to do this.

Iraq, a country that was held together by a family of tyrants, with no history of democracy, not even close to one, and we expect it to flourish there. Afghanistan, a country where the Russians lost so many men they pulled out, we expect to be a democracy, and stay that way. History doesn't work that way, people who don't understand freedom, who haven't fought for it themselves will eventually go back to the old ways, it's all they know. So do we keep propping them up, spend billions of dollars we borrow from the Japanese and Chinese. Were trillion's in debt, not a few trillion, not twenty, but north of one hundred trillion when you factor in all the salaries, pensions, benefits and interest payments, the debt clock says one thing, promises are not included.

Politicians
Liberals and Conservatives

So why do we continue to not only waste money, but American lives in a futile pursuit of world democracy? Simply put we've become blind; our efforts to stop the spread of communism have caused us to believe that democracy is good for all. Factually it is better, but only if a society is ready for it, willing to fight for it themselves, and understand that with freedom there is a cost, not a cost than can be passed on to someone else, one they must pay themselves. Freedom is born, it's not given, it's born from the blood of soldiers of patriots who give all so a country can be free. You cannot give freedom or democracy; you can only provide a platform for it to begin, to take root. So we blindly spend American lives and billions of dollars in pursuit of a more democratic world. Its oblivious politicians are not students of history; it simply doesn't work that way.

Both parties are to blame for this, were not the police of the world and yet, time after time its Americans who hit the beach first, with the rest of the world falling behind. Both parties are only concerned by one thing, they just want to get elected, re-elected and leave office on their terms. As a people we Americans need to stop allowing this, they won't pass term limits on themselves; the only way to do it is to vote them out ourselves. We need to be the limiting factor, to hell with the media, the twenty four seven news cycles and the shiny objects they keep trying to distract us with.

Politicians
Liberals and Conservatives

That's all they really are a distraction, when have you gotten real news without it being spun in one direction or another. Just look at the past presidential elections, you'll see the media slanting one way or another, championing one party over another why? What's in it for them, not the reporters, but the owner of the media company. The reporter is more of a pawn in this, they have to buy into whatever slant is being reported or lose their job. They read a prompter, a script, unless there in the field then they know the rules on how to report and to spin it. In the early nineteen hundreds it was called "Yellow Journalism", not fake news. Its news with a slight bit of truth to it, but not the whole story, it's just enough of the truth so it can be spun to get the people worried or riled up.

Black Lives Matter

Black Lives Matter

So as a white guy from New Jersey how do I write about a topic such as this? I can say all lives matter, is that true yes, but what no one seems to be getting is racism is not dead, not in America today and who's to blame? It's not that easy is it? Can you blame one group one faction of a group; are you then a racist for your beliefs? It's more than that, it's the years of oppression, segregation, being unwanted being pandered to, being kicked to the curb, and it's to borrow a phrase from a friend of mine, "its driving while black"

All the well meaning policies in the world cannot fix what was and remains broken in this country. The lack of civility we have toward each other, it's astounding. Why? Because we're all being split into groups and pandered to. Its big money, segregating society into the haves and have not, even bigger when policies play us against each other due to, perceived societal norms, a white man in a new car in the wrong neighborhood is told to go, leave, and run the lights. Same situation with a Black man and well, the situation become's different, why? Were all human right? So why are they breaking us all up into marketing segments? Simple, it's divide and conquer, politicians care more about votes than problems, even if the problems are systemic in society, they'd rather sugar coat it, than fix the underlying issues.

Black Lives Matter

They'd rather throw money at the problem than actually consider what the base causation is. It's easier than trying to fix the problem, right, if you throw money at it; you're look upon as a fixer even if it fails. Try to fix the underlying problems and you're looked at in a different light.

Color is only skin deep, it's a perception and it is the pigment our bodies generate that give us the skin color were born with. Can we blame the pigmentation for how society reacts to us, no? Can we blame pigmentation for being singled out for any number of incidents, from being considered a possible suspect a wrong doer? No. So how did we get to a point where the color of one's skin, can cause so much angst, can cause so much trepidation that if that person is seen in a certain neighborhood driving a nice car, we automatically assume the worst? What's taken us to this point, where we expect certain members of society not to do as well as others? To be less likely to succeed, to be less likely to have money, cars, homes, nice families?

I will not pretend to understand what a Black male goes through when he sees those lights in the rear view window. I will not infer that he did something wrong, that he shouldn't be in that neighborhood. I am not that kind of person, and I only wish society as a whole had the common sense to see things in the right light. You cannot assume that because someone is different, in any way that that are a possible threat.

Black Lives Matter

People of all colors, races, creeds are successful, we all have members of our races behind bars, so why is it tougher for a black male in society than for a White, Hispanic, Asian, and so on. Have we been conditioned by society to see things that aren't really there? We go to school together, have lunch together, yet they're more likely to get stopped by police than anyone else. Where are we going wrong?

Will I fault the cops? No, while I truly believe it could very well be the training we give our officers that is causing the real problem, it goes much deeper. As were trying to get them understand the neighborhoods they'll patrol, the parents of kids in those neighborhoods show no respect towards them. So is it the perceived slight that changes ones perception or is it the way our society has changed over the years? That I'm not sure of nor am I sure anyone could really answer that.

What I do know is we've create a society where certain children are expected not to perform. They're expected to be the trouble makers, the hoodlums, the dealers, the addicts, the low lives in society. The ones who need more money thrown at them, the poor performers in schools, the ones from the wrong side of the tracks, the ones politicians pander to and do nothing for. What we need to stop doing is blaming one group or another for society's ills. Today everything is broken down; marketing is used to sell us everything. Statistics are used in polls, taken daily on multiple topics, pushing in one direction pulling in another.

Black Lives Matter

Demographics, statistics, records and alike can tell you a story. It's up to you to believe if that story is true or not. The old adage of "Lies, Damn Lies and Statistics" has never been truer, just because a particular group has a higher percentage of doing this or doing that, doesn't mean it needs to remain that way, It doesn't mean it's meant to stay that way and it doesn't mean it's always true either.   Things change over time, just look back at the history of this country, go back further to pre-colonial times and you'll see the only constant is change. Change will come whether were ready for it or not. Do we all need to change? Yes, we all need to wake up and look around, breath deep and see not only what we've been missing, but see the country for what it is, see the politicians for what they are, and fix the problem.

Growing up I was always taught to look at people by putting yourself in the other person's shoes. Not because I was a bad kid, certainly not because we were rich, well off, or high society. My family is made up of Truckers, Fireman, Butchers, Longshoremen and alike; we were and still are very far from the one percent. It's simply common sense, if you want to try to understand what someone is going through, how they may react or if you need to just get a feel for a person, that's what you do. You don't assume that because they're this or that, you need to do one thing or another. You need to look at the whole picture, the whole person.

Black Lives Matter

We look at the police and say they're wrong for this or for doing that, but who makes the rules the police, and citizens have to abide by? Who decides if a certain demographic is to be looked at a little closer than others? Who decides that because statistically, this group is more prone to this than this other group, we need to do this. It's the Politicians, the ones we continually and in most cases blindly vote for. The Police have to abide by the law, same as the citizens of this great country, who creates the laws they need to enforce, the politicians.

So how do we begin to fix or try to fix some of these issues in society? We begin by changing ourselves, our perspectives, not our moral values. We need to see the politicians, for who they are, for what they really stand for and then, decide if we can stand for them. If not, vote for the other guy, don't look at the party, just vote, do the same in each election and you'll see change, it will come quicker than you can imagine.

Why do I blame the politicians? They create the laws; they buddy up with ministers, priests, people who they see as a key to getting elected. They pander, play both sides and do nothing to fix the real problems. The underlying problems in society, nor do they discuss the lack of respect and civility we have for and towards each other. It's so much easier just to throw money at the problem

Black Lives Matter

The fix for this isn't easy, a policeman has literally seconds to decide if you're a threat or not. But if we as a society can start to respect each other and get back to the days of looking out for each other we can make this a better more inclusive society.   We can make the change, simply by doing the opposite of what the politicians, ministers, priests ask us to do. Use your own common sense, if something doesn't seem right it's usually not.   So go with your gut, not your head, not your heart, they can sear you wrong. Your gut, that first feeling you get, the inclination something is wrong, the sickly feeling, that's what you need to use these days.

Taxation

Taxation

We live in a world of super computers, smart phones, tablet computers, smart watches, yet we rely on an antiquated system of taxation, one that relies on regressive policies and does not allow for the class mobility seen in the past. The current tax code is over seventy six thousand pages; do you think anyone in the IRS, Congress or the White house has ever read the tax code? It's hard enough to get Congress to read a two thousand or so page bill, that changed health care as we know it, never mind keep their attention on the tax code.

So how do you change something that's so large, something that has so many special interests clamoring for their deductions to stay. Simple you look at the Country as a whole, not by State, special interest group, or by corporate contribution to your reelection fund, or by demographics. You look at the whole issue, not just a piece here and there. Then and only then can you see the amount of work ahead to reform the basic concepts of an income tax system.

So here's my take on it, we spend hundreds of millions to collect taxes. It costs taxpayers hundreds of dollars each year in some cases more just to insure their compliant with the tax code. That's insane, with the advent of databases and other tools including data warehouses and big data models, there is no need for 80,000 plus employees in the IRS. A much lower number could be staffed to validate the income collections, resulting in cost savings.

Taxation

Since everyone is required to report income that's federally taxable, a reduced staff's role would be simply to validate the data provided. To insure the information is current, correct and entered into the system properly

In fact the IRS gets information from a number of sources, banks and companies to name two. So if we went in this direction with the tax code, and kept it as is and only eliminated a portion of the IRS, you'd still get the information the government needs for taxation. The system would be able to send out a card, no larger than an average post card with what a person owes in federal taxes. Since most people don't update their withholding, for taxes, the majorly of people should just receive a check for the monies owed to them. That would make the system a little fairer, and everyone who's owed a refund would get it whether they filed or not. Perhaps that's why we haven't moved in that direction.

People who are owed money but don't file their income tax don't get a refund. That means the government gets to keep that money, unless you file for the current year and up to three years past. That results in free money for the government, they don't have to go after you, and you don't owe anything. That being said they also don't have to inform you that you're owed a refund, since it's up to you to do your taxes.

Taxation

Why level the playing field and make it fair, after all it's up to the person to submit their tax forms for a refund right? Simple, giving the government free money is like giving a six year old a credit card and letting them loose in a candy store, do you think they'll restrain themselves?

So while they gear the tax system to benefit government, it should not be done to the detriment of the majority of the people. In its current form, the fact that you, have to file to get a refund, even if you don't owe taxes, tilts the playing field into the government's favor and as such needs to be fixed. If they owe you money, they know it and should simply send the check.

The federal government also subsidizes high tax States like New Jersey, New York and others, allowing people of all incomes to reduce their federal taxes based on what they pay not only in income but property as well. While I do appreciate that write-off, especially since they over rely on property taxes to cover schools, local governments and a host of other things. However if we're going to level the playing field, we cannot disproportionally allow for such write-offs. It's not fair to the states that actually have their house in order and don't over tax's there populace. There are a number of ways to go about fixing this, from setting a litmus test, if you make more than a certain amount, say a million dollars or more you can no longer use this deduction, to its outright elimination under the code.

Taxation

Would that hurt, yes, as a member of the middle class and a home owner that would raise my taxable income by double digits, but what's fair is fair. In the end it's up to the people of those high cost States to change the structure of government, to make it more cost conscious. How would they do it? It wouldn't be easy, they have to change the way they vote and start kicking out those who make a career out of politics.

Taxation
Sales or Flat Tax

As I've stated the income tax is a regressive tax, so I for one would like to see it ride off into the sunset. Now doing that will impact a lot of write-offs people get currently. The Mortgage interest deduction would be gone, as would depreciation on goods, inheritance taxes, corporate taxes; we'd basically turn the tax code from the seventy thousand plus pages with special interest deductions, to a two to maybe three page document. That document would cover each instance where the tax would be applied, the percentage of the application, and whether or not a person, making x number of dollars qualifies to have the tax waived.

So how would I propose changing the entire tax system, while maintain services at the federal level? Simple a Sales tax, yes I know people have brought this up in the past, along with a flat tax, and both have strong points. What I'm offering is a standard ten to fifteen percent sales tax or flat tax on everything, the only exception being food purchased at a grocery store and possibly clothing, two basic necessities. So if you walk into a deli and order pastrami on rye with American and hot mustard, yes the tax would apply on top of your local sales tax.

Taxation
Sales or Flat Tax

In my judgment there are a number of better ways to tax than by taxing income. These should be explored and tested. Yes I know playing with the tax code can result in deficits, but look at where we are now, twenty plus trillion in debt, the add pensions and benefits and you more than likely north of one hundred trillion. You'd need one hell of an income tax to cover the repayments on all that money so why not experiment. Saving the American people time and effort to me would be a reward in itself. If you wanted to eliminate the personal income tax and still provide enough money to the federal government that could be done in any number of ways. So let's explore one way that would not only eliminate the personal income tax but rebalance how taxes are applied and collected.

Currently the federal government takes in about three point two trillion dollars, leaving a deficit year over year when you compare debits to credits. That deficit, results in further borrowing and ever expanding deficits. In order to get this under control, the amount of revenue taken in must increase. As such any additional monies collected would need to be constitutionally guaranteed to pay down the deficit.   If such an amendment were to pass, said revenue above the current three point eight or so trillion, would go towards deficit reduction.

Taxation
Sales or Flat Tax

If the increase were say sixty five percent over current revenue levels that would put the numbers near five point one trillion or so. This would allow for one point two or more trillion dollars to be utilized to pay down the national debt. At no point would that money based on the amendment be allowed to be used for anything other than debt reduction.

Taxation
Sales or Flat Tax

Unfortunately a true flat tax or just a sales tax alone may not produce the revenue needed to reduce the debt or eliminate the personal income tax. In order to that and still collect enough revenue we'd need a flat based tax, something like the following;

Flat Tax Rates		Expected Revenue
Corporate Tax	20%	1,002,440,000,000.00
Investment Income	20%	1,002,440,000,000.00
Sales	15%	751,830,000,000.00
Luxury Tax	35%	1,754,270,000,000.00
Home Sales	10%	501,220,000,000.00

While these numbers work on paper, the real world numbers could be higher or lower, depending on the economic realities which may result in other items being added. The percentages are based on an annualized federal budget and are what's expected to be paid by each area; the numbers may or may not be achievable.

Taxation
Sales or Flat Tax

This eliminates the need for a personal income tax, gives the government a cushion and a way to pay down the debt. Are these numbers achievable? Possibly, since depreciation, carried interest along with all other deductions would be eliminated. The sales tax would apply to all transactions, so the purchase of raw materials and alike for products would be taxed along with the sale of the item. As with anything it's all in the way you implement it. It gets the government out of your pockets and you keep one hundred percent of what you earn. You only get taxed on what you spend.

Moving away from income gives greater latitude in tax system. The special interest deductions, mortgage interest for home owners and depreciation on goods from companies would be eliminated, along with a host of others. This would result in everyone paying a fair share based on consumption, not based on income. Now for some this will be a nonstarter as millionaires and billionaires would get to keep their money just like the rest of us. The difference is they'd be paying more in sales tax, as it would apply to everything, including investments.

Taxation
Sales or Flat Tax

Change like these would be a hard sell in congress, after all where do they get all the political donations from? Speaking of those donations, they'd be subject to the tax as well, but I digress. Since both parties get there donations from different groups, special interests, unions, corporations to name a few, it would be a difficult change to make, however no matter how hard it would be, it's still worth the change as it benefits everyone.

Taxation
Social Security

The third rail of politics, entitlements in general but Social Security most of all. Let me start by saying no one is entitle to anything, you have to earn it and with Social Security you do. However the days of the lock box are long gone, much like with State budgets, it's all part of the general fund. Currently you pay six point two percent of your income, and that's currently caped at one hundred twenty seven thousand two hundred dollars. That is if you have taxable income higher than the cap amount you don't pay another dime in Social Security taxes. Why?

At a time when this so called trust fund is being depleted, why in the world would you put a cap on the amount a person or persons should be paying into it? If you're expecting to get something out of it you should be paying in a fair share. To me that means there should not be a cap, this tax should be applied to every taxable dollar you earn. Now I'm no fan of taxes, but if this entitlement is to survive and do what was promised the caps have got to go. It's the easiest way to fully fund Social Security, remove the cap, no changes needed to retirement age or benefits.

It's a common sense solution so why hasn't congress fixed it in this way? Well once again they get money for the election cycle from the very people who benefit from this cap.

Taxation
Social Security

If you made one million dollars per year and had to pay social security taxes on it, it would increase your taxes by sixty six thousand seven hundred dollars and change give or take. Since the numbers are not one sided and an employer pays the other six point two percent, you'd double depending on circumstances the cash flow into Social Security. Now if every millionaire, billionaire and corporation had to pay that additional amount, the deficit in social security would be eliminated and it would be in surplus, resulting in a reduction of the tax for everyone. Easy fix to a difficult problem, but one that's never discussed.

They talk about raising the retirement age or reducing benefits, but never eliminating the cap. You have to wonder do they spend their days on Capitol Hill with their heads in the sand. We pay them to go there and fix the problems, and all they do it seems is cause more. Simple changes like this that would benefit everyone are ignored, and only changes that will benefit the political backers are discussed. Think about it when was the last time you heard a common sense solution to anything from congress? I'd wager it's been a very long time, if ever.

Income Inequality

Income Inequality

Income inequality, wealth gap, whatever you call it is what it is. Successful people make money; they invest it and make more money. So now were not supposed to look up to these people and espouse to be like them. Were suppose to demonize them, they're successful, and most are not, they have ten, twenty or fifty times more money than they'll ever need, we should have that... As a historian that reminds me of a country that way back in nineteen eighteen decided to do just that. They changed the government all be it corrupt from a Czarist regime, to a Communist one. That experiment lasted seventy five years, then in the nineteen nineties it imploded. The USSR is currently still recovering from that seventy five year experiment. One of their noted publications Pravda was wondering in an article back in twenty ten why America is heading down the path very thing they are still recovering from, that has to make you think. People need to take notice, but Americans these days pay little attention to the thought of a Socialist or Communist America, they're too busy watching reality TV programs, that maybe entertaining, but are as far from reality as you can get. We've been conditioned by politicians and the media that a five second sound bit is all you need.

Communism and Socialism espouse that everyone is the same, no matter the education, knowledge or position. This is unfortunately where I see us heading with the idea that success should be frowned upon. At least if you're a Democrat, yet Hollywood, Musician's, millionaires and billionaires support this cause, makes me wonder if any of them are paying attention or if the shiny objects are distracting them in a different way.

Income Inequality

When government starts speaking in terms of income equity, it time for a change. Should people of wealth contribute more yes, most do, should they be taxed more? They can afford it so why not? Simple, the Government as of late sees the citizens more as a cash cow, a resource that can pay its bills no matter how high they go. The Idea that State or the Federal government have a revenue problem and not a spending one is ludicrous. Giving the government more money is like giving your debit card to a stranger. Would you trust a stranger to do what's right having the debit card and pin, with your credit cards? The bigger a government gets the more in consumes the less freedoms and opportunities its citizens enjoy.

Income inequality comes from the very taxation that the government keeps adding to. Income taxes are a regressive tax, they do not allow you to move up in society, they don't allow you to save for your future, and they're a governmental burden put on everyone. A burden where those who have the wherewithal, can benefit while those less fortunate pay beyond their fair share. There has to be a better way to tax everyone at a fair rate, without touching income. There is, but no one in Washington is taking about it. They're all stuck on the wealth gap, the ninety nine percent vs. the one percent. That keeps your eyes off what they're doing and on a politically correct idea that has no foundation in anything outside communism, socialism or progressivism which is by its nature a derivative of socialism.

Income Inequality

Politicians love to talk about a living wage, things cost too much, and you can't have a family on a minimum wage salary. Whose fault is it? Is it the corporations? The business owners? Unions? politicians? Or all of us? In effect it's all of us that cause this, the politicians play on the special interests causing more taxation, we vote for the same politicians' cycle after cycle.

In the nineteen seventies the number of households with dual wage earners, meaning both the husband and wife worked was low. Now for the majority, one income with the tax rates just doesn't cut it. If you add children to the mix, it's even tougher to live in a single wage earner household. So the income tax is a contributor to income inequality, have you ever heard any of them say that, most likely not.

The current education system is another factor in the wage gap. If you grow up in an affluent or semi-affluent area, and attend public schools, it's more likely that you'll go on beyond a primary education to secondary and beyond. Schools in less affluent neighborhoods increase the likeliness that you will not go beyond a primary education. The government and politicians would have you believe it's all about funding, throw more money at it that will fix it. We've been doing that for a long time now in New Jersey and it's not improved, costs have risen, less money goes to the class room, the dropout rate ebbs and flows, but the overall education system still fails those less fortunate. Administrative costs are the largest portion of funding provided to schools. We spend millions of dollars on standardized tests, which tell us little if anything on how a child will perform in the work world.

Income Inequality

We focus on family life outside of school and blame that when a child fails. It's the socioeconomic factor causing these underprivileged children to fail.   They group the children by environmental factors, not taking into consideration the big picture, which includes family life, economic background and education being provided. If you take all three factors into account, you get a clearer picture of what's causing the child to fail. If the family isn't interested in the child's education, the child won't be either. If the child needs to work to help support the family, education becomes secondary. If the conditions in which the child grows up are not conducive to an education, gangs, drugs day to day violence in the neighborhood.   That child unless they are strong and have the backing of their family will fail.

When I was growing up, back in the nineteen seventy's, and wasn't doing well in school, my grandmother and other family members would casually mention the "world needs ditch diggers". Motivational speakers they were not, but I got the general idea and started doing better.   Kids today don't get told that, theirs social promotion, tests that are literally dummed down so more kids pass. Gone are the days of the three R's, Reading writing and Arithmetic are replaced with standardized tests, to which the teacher teach in order for the school to look good. We've lost focus on education and spend far too much on administration, less and less money gets to the class room each year.

Income Inequality

The environment a child today grows up in is far different from the nineteen seventies. They have computers and smart phones; they can search the internet for answers or get help online. Yet today's education system fails most. You wonder why the United States is no longer at the top of the best educated citizens in the world. If you need extra help, who do you turn to? On a Saturday you're not going to find a teacher in school offering additional support. Parents have to dig into their pockets for that, yet in other countries, teachers gladly come in on the weekends to continue a child's education. Those countries are the ones that have leap fogged the US in engineering, science, mathematics and other professional disciplines.

We outsource and insouce people from those countries. Yet we claim our education system is the best in the world, sorry you can't claim that in this day and age, were not even in the top ten countries worldwide for education.

Women's Rights and Issues

Women's Rights and Issues
Abortion

Abortion is a topic that years ago I wouldn't even discuss, being and growing up in a catholic household. Let's just say, as a catholic growing up we didn't speak of it, everyone was prolife, but then in a family the majority of which are males it wasn't a big topic in any case. Today I have a completely different view on it, for one reason or another, but I see it now as a personal choice. This choice any woman can make, for any number of reasons. So for churches and groups to be against something on moral grounds, to me is being against ones personal freedoms, and if free will is something we shouldn't exercise, than the churches, no long need to exist in any of its forms. I still believe in the sanctity of life, that's part of a catholic upbringing. Where politician see an argument for and against, where they would have you abide by their wishes over your own, that's where, I completely disagree with them.

I believe a woman's right to choose under Rowe vs. Wade has been constitutionally affirmed, its basic common sense, the supreme court would not have been able to craft their decision if specific rights had not already existed. If you cannot see that, and I have to admit growing up I didn't, just take a step back, read the constitution and if you do it with an open mind, you'll see it the way the justices did. If you're religious beliefs don't allow you to make up your own mind, I feel for you, your one of the reasons this country is in the trouble it's in.

Women's Rights and Issues
Abortion

Even without Rowe vs. Wade women for years had abortions in secret. All the Supreme Court ruling did was remove abortion from the shadows. It took a practice that was unsafe, unregulated and resulted in a lot of unnecessary deaths and made it much safer. Based on that alone the moral arguments against it, the constant pandering to the base on one side of the other needs to stop, it's getting old. All it does is create a wedge, where a wedge doesn't need to be. It's simply no one else's business, but the person or persons involved.

Lets face facts it take two to make a baby, but the mother has to carry the child, the father is only a participant a provider, protector and supporter, even after the child is born. The woman on the other hand has to deal with much more, she is the vessel, her body goes through changes, she's impacted most, and should be the decision maker. Should the father have input? That's entirety up to her, it really depends on the couple. Should abortions be used as a form of birth control? That's a good question, and not my call, in no way shape or form could I as a male make that decision for a woman, it's strictly up to her. I would hope that for the majority of men, this holds true, if not, you'll need to do some growing up.... If your religion conflicts with your ideals on this, it's time to broaden your horizons.

Women's Rights and Issues
Abortion

The Supreme Court ruled in favor of it, therefore without a constitutional amendment, or an over ride from that court, there could be no change to the ruling. The facts are simple, it is now an accepted process, and their fore for the court to reverse itself it would need to find the original decision in error. That would bring the court under pressure and political scrutiny not seen before or since the land mark case.

So if that ruling remains a litmus test for your candidate, that they'll only support a Supreme Court justice who sees it one way or another, then the rest of the issues in the country must be settled.   They only need to worry about one thing?

If this is all a Supreme Court justice needed to be focused on, I'd agree it should be put it forth before every one. Keep in mind no matter the religion, the philosophy or background of the potential justice or political candidate, they cannot make the change on their own, there are checks and balances, three branches of government and if we can't get them to agree on the most basic ideas, the odds on this ruling changing is slim to none. It should be considered a basic civil right for women.

Women's Rights and Issues
Equal Pay

There is no reason that I can think of, that anyone should not receive the same pay for the same job. Starting salaries should be equal for men and women, and it should not stop there.   If you have two people, with the same education, the same job skills and the same amount of time in that job, I can think of only two reasons why one should be paid more than the other.

In the first case, let's assume that one works five to ten more hours than the other. They're always in the office, working weekends when needed, sacrificing family time at home to insure, project deadlines are met, service calls are answered and so on.   That person, could be considered a high performer, they should make more than a person just doing what it takes to get a general good on a performance review and the standard raise.

Secondly let's assume they have the same education, went to the same college and have the same level of experience for the exact same position.   If one is outperforming the other and is more available then the only difference after the initial starting salary should be the amount of the salary increase due to better performance.   In some companies a good review gets you a two percent increase while in others it gets you less. A high performer in some companies would get between three and five percent in their raise, if anyone is truly getting one. Performance will create a difference in salary, as will availability and a host of other factors.

Women's Rights and Issues
Equal Pay

There are cases where people who go to prestigious schools and get the same degree as someone from a lesser known school, where the prestige employee is paid higher than the other. Beyond the starting salaries, performance and education play a keen role in salary increases. There are any numbers of factors that can cause two people who start at the same company,   in the same role, with the same education, to be on different pay scales.

As long as it's based on experience, education or performance I see no issue here, it's when a woman is paid less, simply because of perceived availability, sexism or due to bias in the performance factors, then it should be raised as an issue. To say that everyone at every level should be paid the same regardless of performance, availability or a host of other factors, put us on a very slippery slope. That slope as the Russians can tell you is easy to get into, and takes years to get out of, it's called Communism and or Socialism, in today's world Progressivism and none work in practice. They sound all well and good, utopian on paper and once you see the real impacts, the ones in societal practice, then it's too late. It does not create a utopian society, it creates a benefit for those who administer it, and removes any benefits for those cast into it.

Women's Rights and Issues
Equal Pay

Everyone should receive a fair wage for a fair days work. There should be no discrepancy in the starting salaries for a woman or a man. If increases are given based on performance factors, they should be clearly defined and attainable by both. If additional education is needed to develop in the role both should receive it. Each person is different we are not robots, we are all not at the same level of education, we don't all perform at the same levels. We are all unique individuals, and if a bias is playing a part in salaries, and promotions, then the management team responsible for that inclined bias, should be removed from the company in question. They should also be prosecuted for their infractions, and back pay provided to those impacted.

Now what I'd like to see when someone talks of the income gap is how they're factoring it. If it's based solely on wages and experience, great split the genders and have at it. If they're adding in maternity leave or rather expected maternity leave and family leave or some other factor that impacts the income of a person. That that is a different topic, people, couples decide if they want to have a family, and that can and usually does reduce the family income, it reduces the income for the mother defiantly. However that is a choice, there is nothing that states you have to be married or have a family. Choices by their nature have consequences. So if you're factoring in choices into a discussion on income, your invalidating you're argument.

Women's Rights and Issues
Equal Pay

You need to have the specific monetary impact of each choice spelled out. Which makes your results subjective at best, you need to have cold hard facts to win an argument, if you're inferring into the result set, then you're contaminating the data, thus rendering it useless.

In essence you need a model, with all the right inputs so someone can check your data. Fact checking these days is more and more important. Otherwise you end up with a for lack of better words, a he said, she said situation. When it comes to politics, not having the numbers, the facts, the concrete data, then you have no basis for the argument. If you can't prove the hypothesis, or provide the supporting data so someone else can back you, then you're relying on Statistics. Something that can be molded into anything you want it to be, so your argument fails.

Women's Rights and Issues
Maternity / Family leave

My wife and I were very fortunate; I made enough money and had the flexibility to be home to help out with the kids. Most families epically those in the inner cities are not, they rely on other family members and with the costs of raising a child, food, and clothing, of course income taxes. How do you make ends meet let alone make a living good enough so you can move up the societal ladder?

When politicians talk fulltime kindergarten, preschool, maternity leave, sick days family leave, they hit a cord with people. They get the feedback their looking for, because it hits a social nerve, people need to work, and they need to work in order to survive. Why? Taxation, a politician has never met a tax they didn't like. It's one of the many reasons it costs more on the East Coast to have a family than say in Texas, but everyone should be able to get the same quality child care. So how do you do it?

Maternity and Family leave is a area where the government doesn't belong. If you decided to have a family, you need to take the responsibility for providing for that family. It's not up to society to raise your child. The "It takes a Village" is only true if you believe in Socialism. When your accepting a job it's up to you to check the benefits the company offers, if they don't offer either of these benefits and you think you'll need them in the future, it's up to you to get a job that has this coverage. It should never be up to the government to provide such services in a democracy.

However with the progressive bent and the fact that we do all want to help each other, no matter what the media says, government is intruding on areas where it really shouldn't. So do you force small companies to comply with a basic maternity leave policy? Do you force them to accept family leave? Are either paid and by whom?

In New Jersey Companies and employees pay into the Family Leave program. While it's nice to have that flexibility, you're not paid at the same wage you would be if you continue to work. Family leave in NJ is about the same as or less than unemployment. So you get paid family leave at a low income amount that's taxable. Nice to have but in New Jersey if you own a home, the amount you'd get via Family leave wouldn't cover your property taxes let alone a mortgage. It would be best to leave it up to the free market to develop a plan, I still remember the days of unlimited sick time that went away back in the nineties but it was a nice to have.

What developed from that was short term and long term disability insurance. Did that make things better? Probably for some companies, since you'd need to use your vacation time prior to the start of short term disability, but it's not better for the employee. Here's where governments and politicians should step in, but they'd rather not upset there corporate donors.

Women's Rights and Issues
Maternity / Family leave

When it comes to Maternity leave each company is different, some don't offer anything others will give you up to a year paid. Should this be left in the hands of the companies or should politicians who, in the majority of cases have never had a real job, to make the determination? Here I think we could use a mix of both, guidelines for minimums wouldn't hurt. In a case where a company offered the benefit they'd have to adhere to the minimums standards set forth by the government. Companies that do not offer it should not be forced to do so.

In both areas Maternity Leave and Family leave it should be the responsibility of the person needing the benefit to plan for it. It should not be the government's role to add benefits for employees of companies, that's socialism or what we call in New Jersey "The Nanny State". Which is what New Jersey has become; the liberal democrats who run the State think they know better than the people of the State and we the voter allow it.

Law

Criminal Law

The United States has the largest population of incarcerated persons in the world. That unfortunately is a fact, it's also a fact that more African Americans are incarcerated versus the total population. There are a number of societal and socioeconomic reasons for the disparity, but that is not the focus of this section. The Criminal justice system as it exists today leaves some defendants undefended. Pro bono or public defenders do not have the same clout as high priced defense attorneys that others can employ. The system, in the way it's structured has lost its way, between mandatory minimum sentences and three strike laws, we've move no closer as a society to fixing our own ills.

Mandatory minimum sentences take control from the Judge and give it to bureaucrats, who know little to nothing about the case or persons in question. There is only one place for mandatory minimums;

In the case of Rape, molestation, pedophilia, incest and murder, a mandatory minimum should be set, but not by a bureaucrat. In these cases the age of the victim must be taken into account, the severity of the crime and life expectancy of the person at that time. No parole, the perpetrator spends that amount of time in jail, no special privileges for good behavior, no time off, and no protective custody. Its common sense, for the rest of that person's life or that families, they will never be the same due to the actions of another, therefore as long as that person lives, or is expected to live the perpetrator should spend their time locked away. It's not about rehabilitation, or the failure there of, it's about justice, plain and simple.

Criminal Law

Why am I lumping these crimes together? They all have the same common denominator; a person's life was taken. Yes the Victim of rape, molestation, pedophilia, incest, is alive, unlike the murder victim. However all of these crimes leave a person scared for life; the criminal has changed the person's state, from what they were before the crime to something else. In each of these crimes, the victim is changed, from the person they were before the event to the person they are to become after. Dealing with the changes, not brought about by themselves but another. So why shouldn't we make it more difficult for those who would destroy a life to spend a defined amount of time in a cell? Why should we allow parole? Does the person who's impacted by a crime such as this get parole from it? Do they get time off for good behavior? No they live it every day, and so should perpetrator of these types of crimes. No special treatment, just general population and let the chips fall where they may.

Voter ID Laws

Since 9/11, the United States has required passengers getting on an aircraft to provide personal identification in order to enter the gate area and board a plane. State governments have modified the requirements to obtain and renew driver's licenses. The IRS requires additional information to insure you are who you say you are when filing taxes. To travel internationally and get a passport you need to provide proof of citizenship, even jury duty requires you in some States to provide a photo ID something as import and if not more so casting a vote, is left open to the honor system.

In order to register to vote, you need to provide a valid form of ID; usually you're birth certificate, driver's license or passport. So why do people, specifically politicians have issues with voter ID laws? While people who are not registered still attempt to vote, the numbers are extremely low so it's seen as a burden a poll tax on the poor and minorities. So why require valid photo id to vote, since the numbers are so low. Simple, we live in an age of hacking, you can hack basically anything connected to the internet so as these voting systems become interconnected we need a way to insure the vote you cast is you're vote. There are people who pay others to take tests for them; as such a valid photo id is a requirement. Who's to say the same isn't true for voting, may be someone decide they don't want to go to the polls and pays a friend or neighbor to go vote for them. It's not too farfetched in our current society.

Voter ID Laws

So how do we make it simple to implement and basically remove the argument that it's a burden? That's easy; it can be done in a multitude of ways so let's start with the most basic.   States control there voter registries, as such when someone registers to vote they in most cases mail in there registrations, some go to the department of motor vehicles others to the county clerk's office. So it's fairly simple to use the new smart licenses most States are now using and link the voter registration to the driver's license.   Once complete, the license could be scanned or the State could simply add a watermark to the license of registered voters that would act as identification. As people renew their licenses, the process would start and be implemented over time.

So you're thinking great, we'll start the process but what about those who cannot afford a car or simply don't drive. In that case where people who don't drive or own a car or have the means to pay for a photo ID, it would be provided to them. How? Sensibly you'd cross check the voter rolls against for registered voter against any number of programs such as Food Stamps, or any number of programs designed to help the poor. Those folks would get a letter detailing the change in process, proving the same time scale as the implementation for licensed driver renewal. So say over a six year period you'd have to go into the elections office, DMV or another State office, and get a new voter ID card with your photo on it.

Voter ID Laws

While this change is being implemented, we make some changes to Federal guidelines on voter registration databases. We start by requiring the States to purge there voter rolls of deceased voters at least two years prior to any Presidential election. Here in New Jersey it's often said the Dead vote and I wouldn't be surprised if a number of them had, it is New Jersey after all. By requiring the purging of records at least two year prior to the election, it allows those who have been removed, if alive to petition the State to be added back to the voter rolls. Effectively cleaning up the systems, making it easier to validate and count each vote.

We then change the system, by allowing for a designation of the Incumbent on every election form. This would require the States, local and Federal government to indicate on each ballot who is the incumbent and who is not. In this day and age people have access to all sorts of things that makes their lives easier, so why not note who the incumbent is, unless there afraid of running on their record, there should be no reason not to support this change. In fact it's probably long overdue as incumbents can masquerade as change maker, when really they're just a tax consuming, non-innovating political hack for lack of a better term.   Maybe Hack is too strong a term, but what do you call someone who puts their political party ahead of the good of the American people?

Voter ID Laws

So as you can see there are simple solutions to Voter ID issues, and notating who in politics has been there far too long.   I look at noting the incumbents as a way for the voter to determine if that person should continue in that office. Since they won't pass term limits on themselves that change gives the American voter the ability to know who's been in office, and determine whether or not based on what they know and have experienced, if that person is still the right one to represent them.

With today's technologies, developing an app for any type of phone, to provide this basic information the, who, what, when, where of politics would seem easy. Looking at today's political system you won't see that app come from any major corporate player. They may mention developing one, or looking into doing so, but they benefit from the status quo. The good of the few today outweighs the good of the many, something that's happened slowly, quietly. Those who can afford to lobby and provide dollars for campaigns benefit and those of us in the trenches, helping to build, improve and move the country forward get screwed.

Gun Control

Ah a topic near and dear to my heart, the second amendment to the constitution. You know the one with so many restrictions it's a wonder you can actually get a permit, never mind a weapon in States like New Jersey, New York, Connecticut or California. These rules and restriction do one thing, cause hardship for the legal gun purchaser.   They have no impact on the criminals that purchase and/or steal the weapons; they don't go through the background checks. As much as the media would like you to think they do, they do not.

If you think the liberals who would love nothing more than to outright ban firearms, are looking to help society get on the straight and narrow think again.   These folks will still have their body guards with permits and exceptions because you know, they're lives could be in danger. While your left to defend your family, home and property with a butter knife or a pair of scissors. Do you think the criminals that use firearms in crimes will be impacted? If you do, I'd like to know what planet you live on? In the history of the world restricting one's ability to defend oneself has resulted in one thing, the failure of democratic process, and its evolution into a dictatorship, or oligarchy. In either case, you lose your rights and the political elite, we'll they get more.

Growing up my grandfather and father were avid hunters, so I grew up around shotguns, rifles and handguns. I learned at a young age to respect the weapon, to understand what using it and or making a mistake with it could do.

Gun Control

 Today kids don't have respect for their parents, each other, teachers, police or firearms. They simply point and shoot problem solved, stolen gun, imported, found or inherited, doesn't matter if the respect for what that weapon can do isn't there, laws banning or requiring registration will do nothing to stem the violence. In fact it would make it easier and safer for criminals to what they do. If you can't defend yourself, you become an easy target for the predator.

        In New Jersey we have Newark and Camden, both cities where the murder rates are higher than the rest of the State and in some cases are the highest per capita in the country. Do gun control laws stop these thugs from killing innocent people and each other? Nope. Have any of them passed background checks? Really? A real question would be why in some states is it easier to get a permit than in others? Why can you get concealed carry in some and in others unless you're a retired officer, ex-cop, private eye or prove by some judicial guideline that your life is in imminent peril; without any of these reasons you've got a snowballs chance in hell of getting that permit.

Gun Control

It's all politics, a hundred or so years ago, you didn't need a license to own a gun, and there were no background checks, fishing, hunting no license needed. So what happened, we let politics into the conversation. Government got involved in something that for more than a hundred years was an unfettered right. They then went about legislating rules creating regulation, fees, and exclusions. One thing I know about government, it's never the answer, more government has never fixed a problem, it only made things worse. Did you know in some States you can lose the right to own a firearm for committing a misdemeanor crime? Yup, there are restrictions placed on a constitutional right, that the founding fathers felt was just and today's career politicians see as a money maker, not just from permits and associated fees, but through fundraising for their next campaign.

In New Jersey for example, it supposed to take no more than six weeks to get your permit. In my experience it took six months, keep in mind however I did not go for a handgun. I wanted the permit so I could get back to hunting, something I haven't done in a while. Still took six months, for something the law states should only take six weeks. When you ask about it, you get a shrug, and I live in a rural area. In the cities it takes even longer and in a few cases, the cities themselves added clauses and restrictions something under the State constitution they can't do. This restricts the law abiding citizen's ability to obtain the weapon, whether it be for hunting, sport shooting or self defense. Resulting in legal fees, wasted tax dollars and time, do they care no, they put the barriers in the way to dissuade you from wanting the weapon.

Gun Control

They think they know what's better for you than you do, and not just with gun control, it's every facet of life, but I digress.

Ever notice after a shooting all politicians on the left can say is we need more gun control, and the right says no we don't. Really, to me gun control is the ability to hit ones target, not a restriction on a constitutional right.

If you're that anti-gun, then obviously you don't want any around you. So let's start with the politicians, the more gun control laws they pass, the less money they should be spending on body guards and security, obviously going by their logic, the fewer guns law abiding citizens have, the safer we all are. So the President wouldn't need the secret service, politicians in general wouldn't need police or body guards, same of the elitists in Hollywood and the music industry. They can be as free as the rest of us. No more guns, even for the Police, they'd have to get by with batons and stun-guns.

Can you see the major flaw? It simply wouldn't work. You could ban, restrict, confiscate what have you and criminals will still get their hands on guns. We don't today and never will live in a utopian society. As much as we'd all like to have no worries, about the basics and more of life, we'll just never get there. One thing's for sure, Politicians tinker around the edges; they do what's easy for them, creating a smoke screen, simply designed for appearances, to pander to special interests, to the benefit of the few, not the many and that goes got both major parties.

Climate Change

Climate Change
Fear Mongering

Growing up in the nineteen seventy's the biggest fear we had was nuclear war. Then around nineteen seventy eight scientists hypothesized that we were heading into an ice age, the time frame for which was hundreds of years in the future.   In schools they taught us that the climate system was a chaotic system that attempting to decipher how one impact relates to another was futile.   In the nineteen eighty's we banned fluorocarbons, a compound found in Styrofoam. This was due to the ozone hole forming in the Arctic and Antarctic. Since that change the ozone holes at the pole's have been shrinking, resulting in the reduction of ultraviolet radiation and its impact on human and other life forms.

Today scientists are receiving funding and pushing the hypothesis of global warming or as they renamed it climate change. I say hypothesis for a number of reasons, the simple fact that those pushing the idea are taking money to say it's occurring, and others in the same field are not very concerned. The climate models are lacking a serious number factors, which are still being discovered, from melt patterns, to waves, to rain fall, the shifting north and south poles along with the above mentioned ozone hole, and any other number of variables. The simple fact that none of the models can predict yesterdays whether, not to mention Paelo climate where CO2 was much higher than today, so why do people believe the data?

Climate Change
Fear Mongering

The lack of overarching data prior to the establishment of the weather service in the eighteen eighty's is a major concern. This information is inferred, and although there have been discoveries of citizen scientists, from years prior to hundreds of years ago, question over not only the authenticity of the data, but the factors and process in how it was observed should be called into question. We don't know the processes they used to collect their data, to me it's anecdotal at best unless they described the processes they used and that process can be replicated today, to see if there is any differentiation. In fact unless all the data is collected and analyzed in the same way across all the countries of the world it's not worth collecting. If you use different approaches, models, tools, data points, and it cannot be corroborated by a second team, you've created anecdotal data, which should be deemed useless.

There is no question that CO2 levels are higher today than at the start of the industrial revolution. There is also no question in that the Earth has been hotter in the past, CO2 levels have been much higher, as were sea levels and the current ice caps and glaciers in the Arctic, Greenland and Antarctic, were not always present. The Earth regulates its own climate, if it could not, then the planet would have never cooled after forming or at the very least it would have formed with a much different climate system and Humans would not exist at least in our current forms.

Climate Change
Fear Mongering

So if the question where, is the Human species causing CO2 to rise in the atmosphere, I'd still say maybe, we do generate CO2, but then so does plans and animals, decaying vegetation, dying trees and alike, it all produces CO2. We are after all carbon based life forms. To believe that the fires that kept us all warm and cooked our food, when were living back in the caves, didn't have an impact on the environment, or the building techniques used had no impact would be ludicrous.

We do impact the environment and having over eight billion people on the planet is having an impact. So what should we do, restrict the number of children one can have? China had a one child policy that caused more harm than any good. Having any government involved in such an endeavor would invite disaster as well. So were stuck so to speak, you could turn off every CO2 emitting device and the impact would be negligible.

Scientists keep focusing on ice loss in the Arctic, Greenland and the Antarctic, each time they come out with a study, they discover a new factor. There are many factors that may affect the retreat process of glaciers, and scientists are still getting a grasp on how they work and interact with one another. They seem to find more things every day from, temperatures at the base of glaciers being warmer than the ice on top, to lava flows and volcanoes beneath the glaciers.

Climate Change
Fear Mongering

Lava movement is a natural phenomena, it's one of the reasons the planet is alive and that the plates pushing and separating the contents cause movement. They site studies and statistics on rainfall patterns from times when no one was even contemplating tracking the weather, by using carbon dating, same for the ice cores.

Since time travel is not currently possible, and probably never will be, these studies need to be taken with a grain of salt, follow the money, who benefits from it going one way or the other? Who is benefitting from the research money?

Then there's the historical record, the early Holocene isolation maximum, a point over eight thousand years ago when the Arctic was ice free in the summers. Yes the tilt of the planet was different, providing more sun thus melting more ice. However during that time agriculture was starting to flourish in multiple areas across the globe. Metal works began, copper was smelted and began to be put to use and animals were domesticated. The climate was wetter, yes, and the Sahara had running rivers and streams, it was populated by animals and humans alike according to science. So during that period of human history, the change in climate was a benefit for all. So the fact is simple, you cannot determine climate shifts based on ice, its expanse or thickness.

Climate Change
Fear Mongering

The past will throw a monkey wrench into you're explorations each time.   Sea shore that remains frozen in time, under the Greenland ice sheet is proof that the ice didn't always exist; it shows wave patterns that were not possible if it had.

The little ice age, is thought in many circles to be the coldest point in the last five hundred years or so. It began back in thirteen hundred A.D. with warm spells in between the start and ending back in eighteen fifty. Since the weather service didn't exist and then, there is no data. At least in the way we started to collect it back then. It wasn't until the late eight teen eighties that weather pattern tracking began; giving us the small sliver of information on which to base a hypothesis. Factoring in that satellites were employed starting in nineteen seventy nine to track sea ice extent in the arctic, you have an even smaller picture on which to base any conclusion. Today we use altimeters to detect ice height and determine mass, if the ice sheet is lower, less mass, higher, and more mass. Here's the problem, the ground below the ice sheet also will rise and fall based upon the weight above and lava flow below, so if the landmass is rising you can get a false positive same as if its falling false negative. Radar is used as well, but it has similar problems, and can't be counted on one hundred percent of the time.

Climate Change
Fear Mongering

So what's the impact if there is no sea ice in the Arctic over the summers, if you base it on today's conjecture, you get Armageddon. If you base it on longer term and historical and geological norms using real science to peer back into the past, looking at the Holocene or other time intervals when ice was not present, it wasn't the end of the world. So does the ice really matter as a measure of climate, would it impact the jet stream, probably. If it's not there it could also cause the Sahara to green once again.

So what's with all the doom and gloom. If you look at things over longer time periods you see the seas were much higher than today. The Glaciers we look at, and fear that they may all melt away haven't existed, in all geological time, there an older phenomenon than humans, predating us defiantly. So once again why?

If you read through articles on Climate Change, formerly known as global warming, previously known as global cooling in the nineteen seventies, there seems to be a pattern emerging. Blame everything you can on climate change, floods, even though rivers have been flooding low lying areas for years. Oppressive heat even thought in the past the Earth has been warmer than it is today.

Climate Change
Fear Mongering

Weather patterns, now this one could be correct, except that while the climate is changing the North and South poles are shifting, which can cause the Jet Stream to change resulting in abnormal weather patterns. Abnormal as defined by the lack of data prior to the eighteen eighties. Since pole shifts according to science happen every fifty thousand or so years, and were in the midsts of one, granted probably near the start more than at the end, we can't discount this having an impact on weather patterns.

The Ozone hole is another factor, once we removed the chemicals causing the holes, in the early eighties, climate changes became more pronounced, could this be the reason for the melt, not CO2? Could it be a bigger contributor than CO2 or methane?

You could look at all sorts of things in the environment and blame climate change, and that's the problem. Unless you provide a big picture, with real details not statistics, not a hypothesis, you're not going to get the results you're looking for. We have hundred and thousand year floods, and when you build near streams, rivers and low lying areas you get flooding. So when so called scientists call out one event after another as being part of climate change, there doing a disservice to the hypothesis.

Climate Change
Fear Mongering

An Incontinent Truth, the day after Tomorrow, both have one thing in common, they lack the real substance people need if they are to change habits. There were so many holes in An Incontinent Truth; it was more like a Hollywood move than the Day after Tomorrow, with its unrealistic climate shifts and the advent of a new ice age. That was more of a farce, but then that's Hollywood.

Scientists like to compare the Eemian and Holocene interglacial periods and base parts of the hypothesis on the climate differences. When in fact the differences make their point mute, climates have cycles, each is different in a multitude of ways, yet they want to try and control it. CO2 levels have been higher during many of the past interglacial periods; each has its own climate variability's and fluxuations. Each is its own point in time, with animals and plants, glaciers and melting, flooding and volcanic activity. So how do you compare them, you can only interpret possibly extrapolate similarities, but that's it, its inference not fact.

So why not follow the money in this case like others? Who benefits if we switch from fossil fuels to solar, wind, biomass, and hydrogen? Who would reap the benefits of that technology? What are the costs associated with it, not just economically but environmentally? If we don't look at the big picture, and establish all the moving parts, were doomed to fail.

Climate Change
Fear Mongering

Imagine the disruption if you were told one day, you can't use your car.

If the government set an edict that all CO2 emitting transportation vehicles were now considered illegal and you must trade it in and purchase a new vehicle. How many people could do that? Drop the car there driving, which would have no value other than maybe scrap, now there's an environmental impact and buy an electric car, hydrogen powered or some other sort of vehicle for transportation? Who would benefit? Banks of course, loans would go through the roof, who pays cash for a car these days? Manufacturers, they'd generate huge profits from the forced sales of the vehicles.

New car dealers, they know the technology so you'd have to bring the car to them for repairs. Investors in those companies and the politicians, who pushed the button and eliminated the internal combustion engine, would benefit handsomely. How? As they usually do, with support for their reelection, donations, Super PACs, and so on. Who loses out? Pretty much everyone else, mechanics would need to retrain on the new technology, if it's not deemed proprietary at first. Car enthusiasts, who like to work on cars themselves, would be out of luck, how do you work around a battery or compound that could kill you or level your house?

Climate Change
Fear Mongering

We could in fact stop using all forms of transportation that emit CO2, or change the way we heat our homes and that wouldn't change anything. CO2 would still rise, climate would still change, and the cycle would continue as it has for all of geologic time.

You can't have it both ways, reduce you're carbon footprint they say, an off they go jetting to the next climate conference. Commercial Jets, no, private of course, you can't have the elitists amongst the riffraff can you? They need their private jets, you know so to show status when they arrive... Please if Scientists, Politicians and United Nations Bureaucrats, wanted to do something real, other than wealth redistribution, they'd start by leading as an example. Until that happens and we see that they're flying commercial to reduce their carbon footprint, until they become the example, the rest of the world will go about business as usual.

They can use their scare tactics, if we go above a certain temperature all the glaciers will melt. Is that a possibility, well yes, is it probable no. Temperatures have been higher than today and life flourished, so what's different today then hundreds or thousands of years ago, simply put wealth. Everyone wants the best for themselves, and no one wants to do the hard work to get there.

Climate Change
Fear Mongering

As a species we should want the best for ourselves, our families etc. However we not all the same, we don't come from the same places, educational background nor countries. Were not robots, we don't live in a utopian world without conflict, without issues. So we set and try to live by agreements that in one way or another fail. By our nature, we are not perfect, we make mistakes, we look at things over long periods without the benefit of facts and try to extrapolate the changes. Without facts, you cannot prove beyond doubt that something is occurring.

Do weather patterns change, does the tilt of the earth change, will the magnetic core changes impact weather patterns. If a butterfly in the Amazon flaps its wings in a light wind, will that cause a hurricane in the Gulf of Mexico? In the latter case probably not but we need remember one important truth. As a species we tend to get things wrong more than we get them right. I'm not saying play the odds, roll the dice and see. What I am saying is science hasn't proven anything beyond the simple statement of climate changes.   Then everything changes doesn't it? Whether we want it to or not, it's something we may have an impact on but overall is out of our control.

Climate Change
Telecommuting

Since no one is really doing anything to prevent climate change, yes government's talks a good bit about it, but other than looking for new taxes; politicians haven't pushed any real plans. As with anything you need some first steps, so let's use the *gas* rationing of the nineteen seventies as an example. Based on your license plate you could fill up on an odd or even day, sometimes you could only get a certain amount of gas, so if we start there to build a plan to reduce emissions it looks like the following;

In order to reduce the amount of automobile emissions, including those from cars, trucks, busses, motorcycles, scooters and alike, you would only be allowed to drive on odd or even day based on the license place you received from the State you live in.   Now constitutionally this would be challenged by any number of organizations including the ACLU. Would this be constitutional, doubtful as you're infringing on the rights of others, it would amount to the same thing as forced car pooling. The embargo in the seventies was a national emergency, it's the only reason the government got away with the odd even rationing. Since we're not at that point, where this would rise to a national emergency, it couldn't be implemented.

Climate Change
Telecommuting

So how do you reduce automobile emissions, if you can't force an odd even model? Technology has evolved to the point where, unless you're in a service industry or manufacturing, you could probably work remotely. That being said the need for office space, or a central office of thousands of square feet is really a relic of the past. Companies have been moving in the direction of telecommuting, at a slow pace, that could be sped up using incentives. Would it be impactful to the real-estate market for Corporate Headquarters? Yes, but not to the economy as a whole. It would in turn reduce other CO_2 emissions, as you wouldn't need to heat thousands of square feet of office space, or need to pave over acres of land for parking. It would initially be disruptive in that people would need to adjust to working from a home based location, going into an office when face to face meetings or gathering required it or utilizing teleconferencing for meeting of all types.

So if the government is so gung ho on fixing the climate, why aren't the politicians pushing ideas similar to this? Money, if they get a carbon tax, that's money in the governments pocket, that's more jobs for friends and associates, family and alike, its more to spend on their special interest friends.

Climate Change
Telecommuting

If they pushed telecommuting it would reduce gas tax collections, reduce toll collections, and reduce the possibility of revenue generators, speeding tickets for one. So how do you implement something that's supposed to benefit everyone, when all politicians can see is dollars?

Health Care

Health Care

Health Care, before we delve into the issues and whether or not government should be involved in the providing of or mandating coverage, let's take a trip into the past, not the distant past, but just after The Great Depression, about the time Franklin Roosevelt was pushing for entitlements like Social Security. In the past American paid for their own health insurance, in fact prior to the early nineteen forties, the majority of people paid out of pocket for medical, not in the way we do now, but directly to the provider. Industries like mining, steel plants and rail roads had doctors on the payroll and on site to help with injuries.

It wasn't until after nineteen forty two, that companies began to provide health benefits. The reason, simple they could be considered part of compensation, with no taxes on the benefit it was a perk for working for a specific firm. The fact that inflation and the war effort was pushing up the cost of labor, made this benefit all the more suited for its time. Congress passed the Stabilization Act which was intended to control inflation, it passed in congress and became law just prior to the end of nineteen forty-two this made the benefit more cost effective for corporations, who were previously competing for workers base on salary alone. Prior to this people bough there insurance directly from, Blue Cross and Blue shield or other firms, when and where they could afford it, selecting the best policy for them based on need.

Health Care

At that point Health insurance began evolving into what we have today, with few changes, or additions beyond dental care. From the nineteen fifties until the establishment of Medicare and Medicate in nineteen sixty five, people either had health insurance thought there employer or paid for plans themselves. Medicare and Medicate were established for low income workers and retirees to receive could receive or continue health benefiters based on their situation. Thus began government entry into a system that worked, wasn't expensive and where people could get coverage.

Little changed until the early 1990s and the Clinton administrations attempts at health care reform. Most major insurers at that time had divisions dedicated to Heath Care, as government began to make changes add new regulations and requirements, companies either sold off of closed those divisions. This resulted in less competition and less affordable coverage with lots of options you pay for but never use.

In Two thousand eleven the Obama Administration signed the Affordable Care Act. Basing it off a system created in Massachusetts. It included a host of options, but you couldn't keep your doctor, even though they said you could. You had to pay for it one way or another either through a Tax penalty for not having health care, payable to the IRS or by paying into the exchanges. When someone in government says "We have to pass this bill to know what's in it", you have to think something is awry and it was and still is.

Health Care

Thousands of people lost the insurance policies they had, simply because they didn't contain what was required by the Affordable Care Act. So if you had catastrophic coverage and that's all you wanted, you were out of luck. You don't want birth control coverage, too bad, pay for it even if you don't need it. It's a one size fits all system, that in its current state will fail over time. The young people, who they needed to join to support the elderly and sick, didn't. They paid the small tax penalty, knowing full well that the law allows you to get coverage when you need it.

Living in New Jersey we already had coverage until children reach the age of twenty six, we also had pre-existing coverage so you couldn't be declined for a preexisting condition. So when insurance companies write policies here they're required to cover a bunch of things in a base policy, thus heath insurance costs more and more with the nice to haves added by government bureaucrats who don't care if you need it, or if you'll ever use it. They wanted it added for some special case brought up by some special interest group and you get to pay for it.

So before I get into how we fix the mess they created, let's take a minute and breathe, just catch your breath. Now think if Heath Care is a right, and not an option or privilege shouldn't companies who sell it be required by law to be nonprofit? Wouldn't that make sense? Who should profit off someone's illness, should anyone? We have all these medical options, so why do they cost so much in the United States?

Health Care

The rest of the world has the same or similar options, and there cheaper Why? Simple, the governments there tell the insurance and pharmaceutical corporations what they can charge or they negotiate pricing to keep costs down. But not here, in the US a hospital can charge up to eight hundred dollars for an aspirin and we wonder why heath insurance costs so much.

So let's start discussing health care in a new light. Currently the Affordable Care Act or ACA has co-insurance at different levels with and up front monthly cost to access that service. So let's say you're paying a monthly fee of three hundred and fifty dollars, with that you get twenty percent coverage until you meet your co-insurance amount of seven thousand three hundred dollars for an individual or between fourteen and fifteen thousand dollars for a family. To support this, you get tax credits based upon your income. Certain devices used in the health care system have a special tax to support this. So take your monthly premium say the three hundred and fifty dollars with financial assistance drops to two hundred and fifty dollars, nice you saved a hundred dollars per month, so over the course of a year you'd pay three thousand dollars. Let's say your annual deductable or co insurance in some States gets reduced by a thousand dollars, so now you're paying the three thousand plus the deductable or five thousand dollars per year for an individual.

Health Care

Even after spending that amount of money, your max out of pocket could be as high as seven thousand dollars above what you're already paid. Subsidies kick in then but your sill paying a lot of money up front for the coverage and who has that kind of money just laying around? I've always found it better to have a monthly premium with twenty percent out of pocket, the way they crafted the ACA it's nowhere near affordable.

So now you're wondering, you have corporate coverage right, how do you know? Simple the plans my company offers conform to the same high deductible plans the ACA requires. So this year, my first experience with it, we've already spent almost eight thousand dollars out of pocket for coverage that's supposed to have a maximum for a family of sixty six hundred dollars. How, some things just aren't covered, every policy has exceptions, and the ACA is full of them, so you max out of pocket may be lower or higher depending on circumstances.

Now with a family say it's the same three thousand dollars for the monthly premium, but now the deducible is five thousand, reduced by the same thousand dollars. This results in a base cost of eight thousand dollars, with your max out of pocket of nearly fourteen thousand dollars. At certain income levels subsidies would be in effect to reduce the cost, depending on your ability to pay. While it was modeled after the Massachusetts requirements, a lot of changes were made, so the ACA is not the same program by any means. In fact if they simply allowed for higher premiums that would offset the coinsurance and deductibles reducing overall costs.

Health Care

In New Jersey this would be considered COBRA, the kind of insurance you try to stay away from, even though with that program you could keep your doctor. It just means you pay one hundred percent of your own or family coverage, which not affordable at all.

Since the ACA went into effect corporations were required to change there benefits packages to more closely resemble it, so you pay less per month on health insurance and they slide in the coinsurance covering your out of pocket expenses to twenty percent until you reach the next threshold. Then your covered on the eighty twenty rule until you max out coinsurance and then obtain full coverage.   So under the ACA companies are required to provide Health Insurance at a certain level, any level beyond which they'll be punished for providing a plan that was deemed too rich in benefits. Unions are in the same boat which puts States at a disadvantage and worse yet taxpayers in those States are on the hook for those costs.

The reason health care became a benefit back in the nineteen forties was to keep wages down, as you read earlier. So why was the ACA designed the way it was? Was it designed to be too costly on purpose? Did the bean counters just get it all wrong or was it designed to push us into a single payer situation? I believe it was the latter, designed so the next administration, presumably democrat could push the envelope into a single payer system with a bloated government bureaucracy at the center.

Health Care

Getting back to the insurance for a moment, if you have to pay seventy three hundred dollars or so to get better than twenty percent coverage, where's the affordability? Coinsurance is just another way to pass on costs from the insurance companies to the insured. I make a very good salary doing what I do in Information Technology and while my benefits come from an employer, getting the full coverage I enjoyed previously is impossible thanks to the ACA. My coinsurance is lower than that seventy three hundred dollar one I quoted from the exchange, but with government incentives the exchange side that may be lower still. But as you can see anytime the government gets involved in something it costs you more.

So let's fix it, ACA out, Single Payer not a chance, the Federal government as well as States have no business in creating a health care system, unless it's not for profit. They all think the one size fits all model will work, and as we've seen it does not. Creating deficits in the name of health care is insane as insane as voting for the same political party simply because its tradition. So we start by removing the Federal government from mandating insurance for all and start to think outside the box. The only place for government in insurance is as a last resort, when all else fails and the market can but will no longer support coverage. That's how the Flood Insurance programs came about, and if you have had to deal with that bureaucracy, just imagine it as a health insurer. We need to start with by taking a pledge from Hippocratic Oath and from *Of the Epidemics*, first do no harm, and move slowly from there.

Health Care

Let's begin the ACA's replacement by establishing that there should be multiple levels of plans. That will not be mandated nor have any requirements outside those chosen by the purchaser. This would be the basement or Tier 0 plan. We live in a free society, you have the freedom of choice so you should be able to choose what plan is best for you and you're family. If this one is a fit, go for it. If you want bare bones coverage this one would be for you, if you wanted coverage for office visits beyond just catastrophic, you could add on to the policy.

We can then start building the basement level so to speak of health plans. The next level or tier 1 plan would have coverage for medical exams, prescriptions and basic options, like wellness care and healthy visits. Costs based on the reasonable and customary payments in your particular area. This basic plan would cover most things, but not everything and you would have to pay more for certain prescriptions, medical devices and hospitalization. In this case you would be covered at twenty to eighty percent for those extra items resulting in out of pocket of costs. Not necessarily the best plan, but if it's what you need, you work with it.

This plan would benefit those who rarely get sick, they'd have insurance and pay a nominal fee but it would be insurance of their choosing not the government. So for this plan, you'd pay a certain amount for the insurance, say two to three hundred dollars per month. You'd then pay twenty five dollars to fifty dollars for an office visit to you primary care physician. If you needed a specialist you'd pay fifty to seventy five dollars, and for urgent care, one hundred dollars.

Health Care

If corporations and unions wanted a richer package, and provide it to employs they should be able to do so. You'll notice no coinsurance for the most part, that's just another way to allow insurance companies to gouge the insured.

They're would be coinsurance for hospitalization only, not prescriptions or office visits, that would fall under the eighty twenty rule, they'd pay eighty percent of all hospital related bills, care and ambulance, you'd be responsible for twenty percent. The plan could also be tweaked to cover hospitalization at one hundred percent, provided the cost was included in the premiums paid, not to exceed fifteen thousand dollars in a given year.

So now we build on the first level or tiers 1, taking all the products included, and place some additional coverage creating the second level or tier two plan. So you want prenatal and well baby care, plus additional well visits and access or you want coverage for contraception or infertility support. You would add these items to the plan you want, and pay the additional costs associated with them.

These costs would be based on your needs, so if you wanted them for one year, you'd pay for a year's worth of coverage, and it would increase you're cost, but you're the one who wants this coverage. This is where the ACA fails, if you want specific coverage's you should be the one paying for them, not everyone else just so your cost is lower, that fails on fairness and more importantly freedom of choice.

Health Care

The third level or tier three would begin as with the first; starting with as basic plan and adding on to it the coverage's you want and are willing to pay for, plus the first level adjusted to your needs. Adjusting the costs with the second level add-ons such as customized medication, immune therapies and other cutting edge care.

So here you'd pay the basic monthly premiums and costs for you're add-ons. Under the ACA this type of plan would be considered a Cadillac plan, where companies and unions would face stiff fines for providing better coverage than the average person can get. We've allowed this for years; all of a sudden we can't anymore, smells like a redistribution of wealth or an attempt to, moving from capitalism to a socialist society. It's not fair and it in no way makes for a level playing field, especially when subsidies are included.

There could very well be more plans than the above, starting with a basic plan and creating an ultimate plan, where you'd pay a lot more than for the basic. But these are your choices; government has no business mandating coverage's, what do politicians know about health care? There not insurance agents, they certainly don't know your situation, financially or physically. Government should exists as a regulatory body when it comes to Health Insurance, should the system fail then they should become the insurer of last resort, not the primary one.

Health care is somewhere near six percent of the gross domestic product or GDP. Do we really want them controlling that much of the economy when they can balance the budget in the first place?

Health Care

Having the coverage on children until there twenty six is a nice to have, but preexisting conditions should not exclude anyone from care. We would be slipping back into a situation where people would lose coverage based on the luck of the draw, and society should not allow that.

While these changes can and do increase costs, the Federal government has the power to reduce those costs by removing barriers to insurance sales. Currently you can't sell plans across State lines, changing that create competition, resulting in lower costs and a bigger pool of insurers.

If they were to follow the basic rules of project management, basic or low hanging fruit first, tackle the bigger problems later, we wouldn't have the ACA, but we would have a stronger heath care system. Think about it, why do people who have a system like the ACA or single payer, come to the United States for treatment? Simple we have the best medicine in the world, the best doctors and hospitals, cutting edge treatments. So why would we want to change that? There are other things we could change to improve it. Basic things that get talked about but not acted on.

Health Care

Taking it to the next level, the Federal government should be negotiating pharmaceutical prices, just like other countries. Why is it, that people order certain medication from Canada instead of buying them in the United States? Cost, that's the driver, if you can save twenty, fifty or one hundred dollars or more buying from outside the United States, why not do so. Why should we continue to overpay for drugs that cost less elsewhere? Where generics are available sooner as well, which use to but doesn't amaze me any longer.

It takes five years just to get a drug to market in the United States, then another five before they'll allow a generic alternative, why? Simple, corporations including big pharmaceutical companies provide a lot of money to the political parties at election time, so they hold the purse strings and we pay the bills I believe in capitalism, always have but with limited government. In a situation that can benefit all Americans, the government should be doing all it can, but within limits. This becomes the good of the may, outweighing the good of the few, it may be a simplistic view but when it's reversed and the good of only the few is taken into consideration, the rest of us get screwed.

So what's so wrong with allowing people to pick coverage's and not have them mandated? Simple, if you can grow government, you do it, they never think outside the box, the only constant in government is spending, never saving money, never paying down deficits or eliminating redundant programs or departments, just grow it.

Health Care

Doesn't matter if you're a sixty five year old female who doesn't need birth control, or sixty five year old male who doesn't need a drug for erectile dysfunction for that matter, it's a numbers game the more they can control the more they can tax, the less control you have.

To put it simply while they call it cost sharing, it's actually the more along the lines of we don't want to do the hard work. We don't want to work out levels and packages, let's just dump it into one package but a bow on in and call that pig a Perl.

Health Care isn't easy, no kidding, that's why every time a government at the State or Federal level starts tinkering in it, premiums go through the roof. That's why you don't pass it in the middle of the night to know what's in it. You need to read the fine print. Bringing in economists and insurance executives to discuss changes to health care is plain crazy, economists know squat about insurance plans they may help with economic impacts. The executives from insurance companies are there for one thing profit, the more government gets involved, mandating coverage the more profit there is for them. It's the law of supply and demand, if supply dwindles and demand rises, costs shoot up.

Health Care

 If we simply change a few of the basics, selling insurance across State lines, you'd see a drop in most people's out of pocket costs, while I don't have real number you could expect better than a ten percent reduction overall, now ten percent may not sound like a lot, but if you spend an average of ten thousand dollars a year on health care, that extra thousand, well that is a lot. Even if you spend a few hundred say five or six, that's still fifty or sixty dollars in your pocket, that's dinner and a movie for some.

The Government claims that health insurance and the lack there of results in bankruptcy, foreclosure and what have you.   So if you take a deep look into the ACA, where dose that series of laws and regulations put a stop to it? Simply put it doesn't it makes it harder for everyone to avoid it with the coinsurance and the myriad of rules around it. Even with subsidies, how would a family of four deal with an out of pocket expense of seven thousand three hundred dollars and only twenty percent coverage? Simply put they'd be in worse shape than under the old system where we paid a set amount each pay period or month to obtain insurance coverage.

I use to pay almost four hundred dollars per pay period, and have prescription coverage with co pays from fifty to two hundred dollars for certain medications. Now those same medications have no cost adjustment until the co insurance is met. In my case that's at eleven hundred dollars per child, not too bad. The medication I use to pay fifty dollars for previously is now well over two hundred and fifty dollars, after the coinsurance kicks in, it drops to one hundred and nineteen dollars.

Health Care

The other medication, I'm not mentioning names simply because it not fair to the pharmaceutical companies, in this case it my health insurance that's causing the price to rise.

This medication I use to pay one hundred and eight dollars for a ninety day supply, with the new insurance, its two thousand dollars per month until the coinsurance is met then three hundred and fifty dollars a month. The generic of this particular medication, while not available in the United States is Canada, a ninety day supply of which costs forty five dollars plus shipping.

So where are the cost savings? Certainly not in the plan my employer offers, other companies are adjusting to conform to the ACA as well, so soon we'll all be in the same boat. Well that is except for the President and some federal workers they remain in the Federal Employees Health Benefits Program, with better coverage then the ACA or corporations provide. Congress got itself a special benefit, not available to you or I, nor the majority of companies. That's something that should never have been allowed to happen, they're not above us, and we elect them not the other way around.

The program if it's kept needs to be modified to force all federal employees, Congress and the President into the same coverage we all have to endure. Since they make a lot more than us, there premiums, annual deductibles and out of pocket costs should be much higher, at least twenty to thirty percent if not more.

Health Care

That will get them in line to fix a program they happily bypass issues with, but left the American public to waddle in it.

This little known exemption for congress comes from a finding of the office of personnel management, granting congress small business status allowing for employer contributions to buy down there premiums on the exchanges. Guess who's paying for that buy down, the taxpayer, what a surprise. Oh and how are they a small business? Do they make money; do they benefit a small group of investors? Do they own a store? Do they produce anything consumable? Nope, Congress in the real world couldn't file as a small business due to its size, it's also a tax consumer not producer so it should not be considered as any type of corporate entity under the ACA, but that would cost them their subsidy.

Now there are a few ways mentioned to fix the problems with the ACA, the start should be small if it's kept at all. I'd prefer if it were scrapped, and people who can't afford health insurance and meet certain income criteria are placed in Medicaid, increase the tax if you must to cover the additional groups but leave the rest of us alone. Medicaid was created for the low income wage earners and the uninsured, so why did we create a new system when adding to the previous with some tweaks makes more sense?

Adults who can work but choose not to, or cannot find a job should receive help as long as they actively search for employment.

Health Care

There are plenty of job training programs and as long as you don't have small children, work should be a requirement for coverage. If you have children over the age of four, in most States the public school system provides preschool, so able body adults with children over the age of four would have to have at least a part time job to qualify for coverage.

Any additional tweaks to Medicaid should start small, as the majority of the ACA participants are in the new expanded Medicaid, so those people remain in that program and the expansion doesn't change. Modifications as they are considered should be vetted out, not just by government accountants but by actuaries across the country, why? Simple, the costs for the plan in New Jersey would be drastically different than Mississippi, same for New York and Louisiana. That's what makes changing the insurance markets so tough; it's much easier at the State level.

Making these changes would allow the rest of us to get the coverage we want without the coinsurance or annual deductibles and unneeded coverage the ACA requires. Now you see why government shouldn't get involved in insurance and a myriad of other areas, all they add is additional cost and time to a process that has worked for the majority of people in a seamless way. People should have options, not governmental mandates for coverage they'd have to pay for but never use. A level playing field is nice, but the good of the few should never outweigh the good of the many.

Health Care

Any governmental program or modification to the ACA should have one additional requirement. All government officials and employees, union and non-union alike, senate, house or office of the president, DoD, CIA, NSA, Supreme Court etc, must be required to and enroll in the new program day one.

In that way, we know the American people won't be short changed, and that even the politicians, have to abide by the new rules, with no special carve outs for congress, everyone pays their fair share, not just the taxpayer.

Since we now know after seven years the republican have nothing up their sleeves to fix the ACA. Nor can they even agree to repeal and replace it on a specific time line; it's time for someone to pull the rug out from under them. They enjoy a benefit, that small business subsidy we cannot get, so that subsidy and approval from the Office of Public Management, needs to go.

The president has the authority to revoke that provision and should do so forth with. Will that benefit anyone, probably not but it will impact the elitists on Capitol Hill and may be just maybe it will cause them and their staffs enough hardship, whether democrat or republican, to actually do something to help the American people.

Who's the Fool

Who's the Fool

Where here, not at the end of a book but what I hope maybe the beginning of change. What you've read and put behind you are concepts and fixes that require only common sense, not a huge lobbying effort, not billions spent by special interests just a change in mind set. While change is hard, it is necessary in order to move forward, you change every day without even knowing it. The cells that you were made up of yesterday have aged and some have died, so you have changed since yesterday, your one day older as such time itself has changed you.

You've read this book, I hope, the daily paper, perhaps even taken a class, your knowledge has increased, that is change. See change is not something that is exclusive to an event, job or action, it's more that the nickels, dimes and quarters in your pocket. It's an overall direction, its movement, time and as such is a daily occurrence in everyone's life. Everything changes, yet most are afraid of it, try to avoid it and fail each time.

My career focuses on change and how to manage it, plan for it and insure the orderly implementation of change. In life it's not that easy, were pulled in all directions by political parties, the media, Hollywood, religion and on and on. They want you to focus on what's beneficial for them, what they believe in, the few, not you or the many around you.   Do you ever ask yourself do they really care? Probably not, they don't even know you but they count on you following them, accepting what they think is good for all and blindly doing what they want.

Who's the Fool

One of the many bands I like, the singer and it seems the majority of the band is pro in one direction, I won't get into who they are or what they believe, but it doesn't mean I don't listen to their music or attend concerts. When they start the political speak, I walk away, go hit the rest room, grab a beer or just go for a walk around the venue. To me, political speech has its place and it's not at a concert, unless it's billed as a political event. In stories or songs that's fine, but I'm not paying to hear an opinion. I'm paying to hear the band play and the singer sing the songs I like, not to hear a political speech no matter how short or one sided. If both sides were addressed it still would not be the place for this type of discussion, that requires two parties to communicate, when one holds the audience and the other is nowhere to be found, there is no political discourse, there is only an attempt at indoctrination.

Now does that mean I don't follow them because of their political leanings? Nope, same with an actor in Hollywood, could care less who they're pitching for or voting for, doesn't impact me or you for that matter. Would I attend and event for a meet and greet, the event being political, definitely not, but I'll still watch the movies, TV shows etc. There persona is there for entertainment, not politics, what they do as a celebrity or in their private lives has no impact on what I think or believe. I'm not an ostrich, I don't burry my head in the sand, and hope everything goes well. I participate, learn what I can, and make my own decision based on the information provided by any number of sources none of which are the main stream media. Does that mean I research everything about a candidate prior to voting?

Who's the Fool

Nope, I do check their voting record, but the vast majority of the time, I vote in the other direction, if one parties in power for example, if they're not up to snuff I vote for the other guy or gal.

When I started writing this, it was just before the twenty sixteen election cycle. Listening to both sides make fools out of themselves in the hopes they'd be the one elected. Neither candidate was what I would call optimal; they both had their faults, issues and infractions. As for third party candidates, the media hardly covered those options at all and only did when a candidate made a mistake or misspoke   But when you put yourself above others, you disregard policy and in another country espouse the benefits of outsourcing American jobs as if it doesn't hurt anyone, that's a person I cannot vote for. Never mind the fact that having a personal server with classified government information on it in your home is a violation of so many policies, to many to name here, is a blatant disregard for your position in government and your security clearance.

Why would I look at the email issue and not let it slide? Easy I've had that security training. It's not a short class, mine was over the course of two days, with very specific details on what would happen if any classified information was discussed, emailed, improperly handled or viewed in public, while in your custody. Now if my low level security briefing was that detailed, that specific, I find it hard to believe that the one given to the Secretary of State would be any less. Whether you have time in government service or not, its common sense, those icons

Who's the Fool

on the email mean something, you don't read or respond to them outside a secured room, on a secured network.

To me it doesn't matter who you are, how long you've been in government, who you know etc. That's trivial, when you don't follow the rules people, real people can get hurt, and that's something you cannot take back with an apology. People have gone to jail for less, even when they used the information to save lives, so the punishment that they received should be doled out to anyone who breaks the rules. No one, not the Secretary of State, Speaker of the House, Senate Majority leader, Vice President or the President is above the law.

While the President has the power to declassify information, if it's shared prior to being declassified, outside a secured room or with people who should not have access to it, he or she should be held accountable as well. The law is the law and no one should be able to wiggle around or by pass the consequences. If the law applies to a buck private in a warzone, a contractor on a military base or general in the pentagon, never mind numerous others. Then politicians don't get to exempt themselves or get a pass at any level, if anything once you receive that security briefing and see that classified information, if you leak it, have someone leak it or expose it in any way, the consequence of the violation should be applied. The longer you're in office at the time of the infraction, the more time you should spend behind bars.

Who's the Fool

Not to mention the fact that the democrats were acting like the election was a formality. Barges in the east river of Manhattan for fireworks, really why not call in a few matching bands and have a parade scheduled as well? One way to lose at anything is to act like one piece of it; in this case an election is a formality. Ask the New England Patriots, in two thousand seven they were eighteen and zero, going into the super bowl.   The players according to some were inviting the New York Giants players to their parties after they won. Just one problem, they didn't win, was the invite enough of a boost for the Giants, did give them an advantage or did they just play better? Who knows, but after that game, the assumed super bowl champions were eighteen and one, and the New York Giants were super bowl champions.

The quickest way to defeat is to plan for only victory. The way the candidate was portrayed may have influenced some, but it sure turned off a lot of people. Wining the popular vote is a hollow win, it takes the Electoral College, two hundred and seventy or more votes to get elected. So while being popular is nice it takes the Electoral College to decide the winner. It was setup that way so popularity would not be the only factor in the election, insuring smaller States had the same weight as larger ones.

The second option during the election was the current President, is he perfect? No but as most of the country outside New York, New Jersey, Connecticut, California and a few other States knew, it was time for a new direction a change.

Who's the Fool

The previous administrations, notice I'm not blaming one, it goes back to the late nineteen eighties did little to nothing besides cost American citizens jobs, through countless regulations, free trade deals and outsourcing jobs for pennies on the dollar. Has he stepped into controversy? Yes a few time too many, but he's not a politician, he's a business man, so I expect a mistake here and there. Do I accept it, no. Do I agree with what he says all the time? No, you probably don't either and that a good thing, you're thinking for yourself.

So whenever that happens, when you and that politician who represents you don't see eye to eye, put a check mark in your win column, and if you agree with a politician, give them a check mark, see who's doing better month to month. You could use that the next election cycle as a point of reference to see where you stand against the politicians. Does that guarantee they follow that they said last time around, nope, but it does give you something to use as a determining factor with each election. The chart could look something like the once included;

Who's the Fool

Me	Politian A	(Dem, Rep, Other)	Politian B	(Dem, Rep, Other)	Politian C	(Dem, Rep, Other)

You may find over time you agree less with the person you voted for and more with someone else. It's a good way to check yourself, get you to see and think a little more clearly when it comes to voting and for whom. It's up to you, but clarity in ones positions is a benefit, feel free to add or modify the idea, just putting it out there as an option. You may even find that the party you've been supporting is no longer a fit for you and that the other is or perhaps you'll find that neither major part fits with what you believe and that an alternative party might be best. That's not a bad thing, having options is always good, too many may not be at times, but when you get down to it, what's more important, you're beliefs and ideals, that shape this great country, or the politicians job? I dare say, you and you're future are more important than them.

Who's the Fool

Politicians would see this as the other way around that the job they do requires a background in politics that the average American would have no idea how to do the job that they do. When in fact it is truly the other way around, we have no need for politicians, the founding fathers knew that. George Washington wanted a participation based democracy, very different from the one we have today. One where the people, not those of one elitist group or another worked to keep the country free and moving in the right direction, drawing lots in the town square. One where your neighbor or you could be called to serve for that period of time. Obviously the politicians of the day didn't take kindly to that idea and we ended up with that we have today.

We all want to be on the winning side, voting seems to be no different to most than choosing your favorite baseball or football team. Looking at it at that level it becomes a problem, believe it or not. The problem is; if you vote based on that mind set, and not consider other variables, you end up in a constant quagmire a swamp so to speak. A place where the same people promise the same things over an over and do nothing, the status quo, or swamp whatever you want to call it.. Repeal and Replace, for one example, republicans had seven years to come up with a strategy. Where are they, lost in the wilderness of politics and in fighting.

Who's the Fool

If either political party really wanted to fix things they'd take smaller bites, go for the low hanging fruit, open the insurance markets across State lines, see how that reduces rates then, and only then start tweaking other things. If you recall growing up, if you ate to fast you mother would tell you to chew your food, same in politics, try to move to fast and you won't digest the changes right, and what comes out in the end may not be what you expect. All they do however, is tinker around the edges, and never address or fix the real problems. People seem to know this, when you ask them, yet these same people vote for that same politician.

If you've ever done budgeting, you know better than to attach a Christmas list, a new car, a fur coat, a house what have you when you don't have the money for it. Yet politicians do this all the time, they bloat the budget and while the President has the line item veto, it seldom used as a line by line clean up. So why do we have to budget in reality and they budget in a fantasy world? Simple, we're the cash cow that supplies the taxes to support the spending. Should your income be taxed at all? Or should we use a consumption or sales tax? I'd prefer a sales tax, it less intrusive and let you keep your money. Something the elitist politicians at every level would fight tooth and nail over, yet it's the fairest way.

Who's the Fool

      Looking back to the seventies and early eighties before the twenty four hour news cycles,   the news was the news, no opinion or inference just the facts. Today everything in the media seems to be biased one way or the other for local as well as national news. When opinion slips into news it's no longer journalism, you polluting the facts, and trying to get others to see it from your side. The only goal there is viewership, ratings so your channel, paper, magazine or website can get more advertising, it's less about the topic and more about the perception and that's not news that's what they called yellow journalism back in the early nineteen hundreds. News becomes opinion, speculation or worse sensationalized and moves further away from fact all in an effort to sell more copies, truth be dammed.

      If you've ever been distracted from the real news of the day you're not alone, they use of a myriad of distractionary tactics, seems to be part of the program now. News isn't just news anymore it contains minimal fact, just the basics with a wrapper around it. The News has become performance art, where shiny objects, people and locations are used, to distract the viewer from the real news and provide a lesser substitute. It's not just the equivalent of yellow journalism from the early nineteen hundreds is there version of political correctness, which means you never know what they really mean and have to infer it for yourself. Is that a bad thing? Yes, unless you have all the facts you end up with an opinion on something where the basic premise is incorrect, I'd rather have just the facts, than the reporters or news anchors interpretation of those facts.

Who's the Fool

Think about that for a minute, you're in charge of a large project, program, sale or purchase. Your boss has asked you to provide a presentation covering everything from the day one start to where you are today. Now if your behind he already knows it, his bosses who your presenting to might not, but imagine if he told you to leave out this or that, paint a rosy picture, there are no issues, everything is ahead of schedule, the buyers are paying top dollar, the project is ahead of schedule, the program is almost complete etc. How would you feel? Could you leave out pertinent facts to squeue the presentation? In the end, what do you thing would happen if what you were working on suddenly came to a screeching halt? Once the post modem was done, do you think you'd still have a job? That's the way it should be in the media, but unfortunately it not, each network leans one way or the other and it up to us to decipher the real news.

Before we get into why the title, let's take a little test; simply note a yes or a no for each of the following questions. It's not a real test; no one will come to your home and collect your answers. It's a way for you to get insights into yourself and your voting habits nothing more. So before you move to the next page of this book, take a few minutes and write down the answers, be honest with yourself. Put it on a separate piece of paper, or just note it in the book after all you own it. Use it as a reference just like the Eye to Eye chart; your answers may surprise you.

Who's the Fool

1. Are you now or have you ever been a member of a political party? (Yes / No)

2. Have you voted consistently for one political party over another? (Yes / No)

3. Have you consistently voted for the same political candidate? (Yes / No)

4. Have you ever considered voting for a different political party or candidate? (Yes / No)

5. Do you believe the media should play a role in politics? (Yes / No)

6. Do you believe media coverage is always fair to both political parties? (Yes / No)

7. Do you believe everything the media tells you? (Yes / No)

8. Have you voted the same political party simply because other people wanted you to or because for generations your family has? (Yes / No)

9. Do you believe that both political parties put the best interest of American Citizens ahead of party politics? (Yes / No)

10. Do you want to drain the swamp in D.C. and enact real and meaningful change? (Yes / No)

Who's the Fool

Now look over your answers, if you answered yes to the first six questions, take a walk down memory lane, not an actual lane but the stored memories in your mind. Looking at those questions, did you benefit from anything related to them? Did others you know? Or did no one benefit? It's hard to tell isn't it? But that wasn't the purpose of the questions, they were there to open your mind to the fact that you're more than likely following the herd and you don't even realize it.

My grandfather worked in a slaughter house, so growing up I got to see animal behavior first hand. Its and experience let me tell you, especially when your all of three years old. It's what the herd mentality does; it leads you like the black sheep leads a herd in to the slaughter only to exit the building on the other side.   The other sheep, the followers they go to slaughter. The black sheep, they're put into another flock, and on it goes kind of like politics or political parties.

We let them lead us and blindly follow, it's because of us they have the positions they do. Yet they believe there indispensable in a lot of cases, really? Who can't be replaced now a days, everyone who's gone through life has see someone or something replaced in it. When technology changes, things get replaced, look at the smart phone, it's literally replaced twenty or more devices we took for granted. So why do politicians think there not replaceable?

Who's the Fool

Look at what you do every day at work, at home, in life. Do you believe that any facet, of your day to day life is without politics? You know how to negotiate, how to wheel and deal, so the only difference is they do it for a living and you do it as part of life. In the grand scheme of things, politicians are really only good for one thing, in my mind, and so as not to pollute yours, I leave it up to you to decide what the one thing they're really good is.

So who's the fool? In essence we all are, thinking that one party is different from the other. That the special interests that support one candidate aren't hedging there bets and actually supporting both behind the scenes. Politicians made themselves at home, they like their cushy jobs, they show up around election time each cycle, make promises, that they may or may not intend to keep. They get to rub elbows with other elitists while we sit back, get distracted and allow them to be in the office well beyond their usefulness.

So while were all the fools that continually vote for the same politicians, we can change that. We don't need government to tell us how to live, to monitor our every move, to tax us beyond comprehension and to grow beyond need. We need to simply wake up and take back what the politicians have been taking from us. We need to change and through that change, they'll be forced to. Politicians will never pass term limits on themselves; we have to be the limiting factor.